CHILDREN'S ENCYCLOPEDIA OF SCIENCE

Giles Sparrow

Picture Credits:
Every attempt has been made to clear copyright. Should there be any inadvertent omission, please apply to the publisher for rectification.
Key: b–bottom, t–top, c–center, l–left, r–right
Alamy: 26-27 (David Fleetham), 114-115 (Greg Vaughn), 115cr (Xinhua); **Arcturus Publishing Ltd:** 44br (Stefano Azzalin); **CERN:** 82-83 (Daniel Dominguez/Maximilien Brice); **ESA:** 94-95; **ESO.org:** 119tr; **FLPA:** 40-41 (Frans Lanting); **Getty Images:** 76-77 (Education Images/UIG); **Lawrence Livermore National Laboratory:** 100-101; **Library of Congress:** 85tr (Oren Jack Turner); **NASA Images:** 15br, 71cr, 80br (JPL-Caltech), 85c (ESA/ Judy Schmidt), 98cl, 118cl (SOHO/ESA), 120c, 122br (ESA/Hubble Heritage Team), 124c (WMAP Science Team), 125bl; **NOAA Photo Library:** 38cr (Lost City 2005 Expedition/OAR/OER); **Pikaia Imaging:** 120-121; **Science Photo Library:** 1 (Jellyfish Pictures), 4-5 (Photo Insolite Realite), 9cl (Tony McConnell), 10cl (Dr Gary Settles), 12l (GIPhotoStock), 18-19 (Matthew Oldfield), 22-23 (Patrice Loiez, CERN), 30tr (Kateryna Kon), 40c (Smetek), 44-45 (Jose Antonio Penas), 60-61 (Jellyfish Pictures), 64-65 (Zephyr), 65tr (Mauro Fermariello), 73br, 84-85 (Nicolle R Fuller), 86b (Universal History Archive/ UIG), 90-91 (David Parker), 92-93 (Samuel Ashfield), 92cl (US Army), 96tr (Dr Gary Settles), 98-99 (Pascal Goetgheluck), 102-103 (Nicolle R Fuller), 102cr (Philippe Plailly), 104cr (Equinox Graphics), 104br (Gusto Images), 108cr (Planetary Visions Ltd), 109br (Spencer Sutton), 111cr (Carlos Clarivan), 112cr (Gary Hincks), 114cr (Henning Dalhoff), 117b (Mark Garlick), 118-119 (NASA/JPL), 120-121 (Chris Butler); **Shutterstock:** cover main (Sebastian Kaulitzki), cover (top row, various), 4tr (adriaticfoto), 4c (Neal Pritchard Media), 4br (YC_Chee), 5tr (adike), 5br (NASA Images), 6-7 (ZinaidaSopina), 6tr (MicroOne), 6bl (sandatlas.org), 7bl (kaer_stock), 8-9 (Sebastian Janicki), 8cl (grafvision), 9bl (Macrovector), 10-11 (Digital Storm), 10bl (MilanMarkovic78), 11tl (Evgeniya Chertova), 12-13 (Fredy Thuerig), 13cr (Inna Bigun), 13bl (NoPainNoGain), 14-15 (Maximilian Laschon), 15tl (NoPainNoGain), 16-17 (Mark Agnor), 16tr (Sebastian Janicki), 17tl (yongyut rukkachatsuwa), 17bl (Andrey_Kuzmin), 18cl (Taras Vyshnya), 18bl (Designua), 19bl (CE Wagstaff/Georgios Kolidas), 20-21 (cyo bo), 20tr (haryigit), 21cr (patx64), 22bl (Andrea Danti), 23cr (MichaelTaylor), 23bl (mila kad), 24-25 (Protasov AN), 24bl (Inna Bigun), 25br (Larina Marina), 26cr (Lightspring), 26bc (Susan Schmitz), 28-29 (hamdee), 28l (Calmara), 29cr (koya979), 30-31 (ranjith ravindran), 30c(Designua), 31cr (Designua), 32-33 (Brannon_Naito), 32cr (Sakura), 32br (Molly NZ), 33bl (BlueRingMedia), 34tr (tcareob72), 34trbl (hillmanchaiyaphum), 34trbr (Popova Tetiana), 34ct, 34ctr (schankz), 34c (Andrey Armyagov), 34cbr (F Neidl), 34cb (Gerald Robert Fischer), 34bl (dangdumrong), 34br (Jolanta Wojcicka), 35tlb (Romeo Andrei Cana), 35tc (Victor Tyakht), 35tr (Zety Akhzar), 35ct (Rich Carey), 35ctr (Salparadis), 35cb (scubaluna), 35bc (Rich Carey), 35 br (Laura Dinraths), 36-37 (sebi_2569), 36cl (Bildagentur Zoonar GmbH), 36bl (Christos Georghiou), 37cr (yougoigo), 38-39 (Miami2you), 39tl (Budimir Jevtic), 39br (Sebastian Kaulitzki), 41bl (MatiasDelCarmine), 42-43 (Hedrus), 42bl (Esteban De Armas), 43tl (Panda Vector), 44cl (Tatsiana Salayuova), 45bl (kalen), 46-47 (Sirisak_baokaew), 46cr (Sebastian Kaulitzi), 46bl (eenoki), 48-49 (Life science), 48cl (Christos Georghiou), 48bl (NotionPic), 49br (VILevi), 50-51 (Biomedical), 50tr (NoPainNoGain), 50bl (stihii), 51bl (LynxVector), 52-53 (adike), 52tr (yodiyim), 52c (wavebreakmedia), 53bl (Tefi), 54-55 (Michal Knitl), 54cl (Tefi), 55cr (Robert J Gatto), 55bl (Everett Historical), 56-57 (Nerthuz), 56cl (nobeastsofierce), 56bl (EstherQueen999), 57r (Xray Computer), 58-59 (Sebastian Kaulitzki), 58cl (deepadesigns), 58cr (Designua), 59cr (Sebastian Kaulitzki), 59bl (Panda Vector), 60c (Tefi), 60bl (Double Brain), 61br (Olya Vusochyn), 62-63 (Juan Gaertner), 62c (Kateryna Kon), 62bl (GraphicsRF), 63br (by pap), 64c (royaltystockphoto.com), 64bl (Designua), 66-67 (3Dsculptor), 66cr (Sombat Muycheen), 67bl (freevideophotoagency), 68-69 (Cassiohabib), 68cr (Roberto Cerruti), 68c (JonathanC Photography), 68bl (StockSmartStart), 69 cr (Aspen Photo), 70-71 (Sky Antonio), 70c (TES_PHOTO, MatiasDelCarmine, Genestro), 70bl (MatiasDelCarmine), 72-73 (Little Dog Korat), 72cl (Kosta Iliev), 72bc (pandapaw), 73tl (Morphart Creation), 74-75 (Gabor Kenyeres), 74tr (Littlekidmoment), 74c (SkyPics Studio), 74bl (Fouad A Saad), 76c (Zigzag Mountain Art), 77br (ShutterStockStudio), 78-79 (Kobby Dagan), 78cl (kasezo), 78bl (MatiasDelCarmine), 80-81 (Jag_cz), 80tr (Fouad A Saad), 81tl (ALXR), 82bl (Ayon Tarafdar), 83tr (GiroScience), 85bl (Meowu), 86-87 (Maryna Kulchytska), 86tr (SherSS), 87bl (NPaveIN), 88-89 (mekcar), 89cr (andrea crisante), 90c (fotografos), 90bl (Luisa Fumi), 91br (tomas devera photo), 93tr (Volodymyr Krasyuk), 94bl (Chris Singshinsuk), 95cr (asharkyu), 95bl (Blan-k), 96-97 (satit_srihin), 96bl (Peppy Graphics), 97bl (Gabor Miklos), 98bl (AF studio), 99tr (Thongsuk Atiwannakul), 100c (Martin Lisner), 100bl (Blue Ring Media), 101bl (udaix), 102tr (Forance), 102bl (Shmitt Maria), 104-105 (Marcin Balcerzak), 105tl (science photo), 105bl (Pogorelova Olga), 106-107 (Vadim Sadovski/NASA), 106tr (Diego Barucco), 106cr (Marc Ward/NASA), 108-109 (Therato), 108bl (Palau), 110-111 (Harvepino), 110c (sumikophoto), 110bl (NoPainNoGain), 112-113 (Jakub Cejpek), 112bl (M Scheja), 114bl (robin2), 116-117 (godrick, vovan/NASA), 116cl (Castleski/NASA), 116bl (Monkey_Fish), 120tr (Designua), 120bl (Maria Zvonkova), 120cl (vectortatu), 124-125 (Andrea Danti); **thehistoryblog.com:** 29bl; **Wellcome Images:** 47tl; **Wikimedia Commons:** 21tl (Christian Albrecht Jensen), 25tl (Nobel Foundation), 27tl (Alexander Roslin, Nationalmuseum, Stockholm, Sweden), 30bl (Robert Hooke, *Micrographia*, National Library of Wales), 35tl (Maija Karala), 40bl (Charles Darwin and John Gould: *The Voyage of the Beagle*), 43br (Mendel: *Principles of Heredity: A Defence*/ Bateson, William), 66bl (Justus Sustermans, National Maritime Museum), 76bl (Frederick Bedell's *The Principles of the Transformer* (1896)), 79tr (Niabot), 89tl (www.jedliktarsasag.hu), 92bl (Science Museum, London/Mrjohncummings), 106bl (Davorka Herak and Marijan Herak), 113bl (Scottish National Gallery/Henry Raeburn), 118bl (Adler Planetarium and Astronomy Museum, Chicago/Brahe's *Astronomiae instauratae*), 123bl (Harvard University Library).

ARCTURUS

This edition published in 2018 by Arcturus Publishing Limited
26/27 Bickels Yard, 151–153 Bermondsey Street,
London SE1 3HA

Copyright © Arcturus Holdings Limited

In this book, one billion means one thousand million (1,000,000,000) and one trillion means one million million (1,000,000,000,000).

ISBN: 978-1-78828-507-0
CH005808US
Supplier 26, Date 0318, Print run 6203

Consultant: Dr Mandy Hartley
Author: Giles Sparrow
Editor: Clare Hibbert @ Hollow Pond
Designer: Amy McSimpson @ Hollow Pond

Printed in China

CHILDREN'S ENCYCLOPEDIA OF SCIENCE

CONTENTS

Introduction

Science is amazing! It shapes our understanding of the Universe and has transformed our everyday lives. At its heart, science is a way of collecting facts, developing ideas to explain those facts, and making predictions we can test.

Laboratory Learning

Chemistry investigates materials, from solids, liquids, and gases to the tiny atoms that make up everything. By understanding the rules behind how different kinds of matter behave, we can create new chemicals and materials with amazing properties.

Observing a chemical reaction under a microscope

Secrets of the Universe

Physics is the scientific study of energy, forces, mechanics, and waves. Energy includes heat, light, and electricity. Physics also looks at the structure of atoms and the workings of the Universe. Even the galaxies obey the laws of physics!

Many forms of energy are involved in a storm.

Chimpanzees, one of around 7.8 million species of living animals

Life on Earth

Natural history is the study of living things—the countless plants, animals, and other creatures that inhabit Earth now or which existed in the past. It studies how these organisms are influenced by each other and their environment. It also looks at the complex process of evolution—gradual change from one generation to the next.

Electron microscopes let biologists study creatures such as this headlouse in extraordinary detail. The microscope itself is the result of a scientific breakthrough in the study of subatomic particles (see pages 24-25).

How Organisms Work

Every living thing on Earth is made from cells—individual units that can combine and work together to create incredibly complex systems, including human beings. Biology involves the study of cells, and also the many tissues and organs that go into creating living things.

Biologists look at the workings of the human body.

Earth and Space Sciences

Geology is the study of our planet, Earth—how it was made, what it is made of, and how it has changed over time. Astronomy, meanwhile, looks at our place in the Universe. It examines how Earth, the solar system, and other objects in space behave—as well as how the cosmos began, and how it might end.

Our planet, Earth

Phases of Matter

Matter is the stuff that makes up the Universe. It is built from countless tiny particles called atoms and molecules. Depending on how these particles arrange themselves and join together, matter can take one of three forms: solid, liquid, or gas. These forms are called phases.

Material Bonds

Solid substances are made up of particles joined by strong, rigid bonds. Particles in liquids have looser bonds, which constantly break and reform. Gases are very loose collections of atoms or molecules that have extremely weak bonds. The strength of a material's bonds affects its ability to keep its shape.

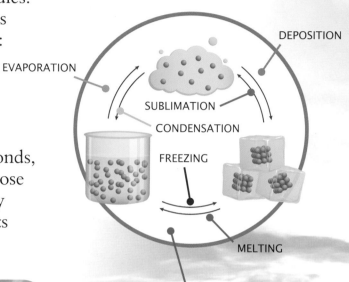

DEPOSITION

EVAPORATION

SUBLIMATION

CONDENSATION

FREEZING

MELTING

Water can be a solid (ice), liquid, or gas (steam). When it's solid, it stays the same shape whatever container it's put in. As a liquid, its molecules flow outward to spread across surfaces. Steam spreads to fill its container or heads in all directions.

Changing Phases

The phase of a substance is affected by how much energy its individual particles have to move around, and this energy depends on the material's temperature. Heating a solid material enough loosens its bonds and makes it melt. Heating a liquid will cause particles to boil or evaporate into a gas.

Different substances have different melting and boiling points. The melting point of rock is very high, so molten lava rapidly turns solid when it erupts from a volcano and begins to cool.

DID YOU KNOW? The metal mercury is usually in liquid form. Its freezing point is –38.8°C (–37.8°F) and its boiling point is 356.7°C (674°F), both the lowest of any metal.

A geyser is created where matter suddenly changes its phase.

As the steam meets the cold air above, it cools and turns back to liquid water droplets.

Wherever the water finds a way through cracks to the surface, it suddenly and violently boils into steam.

Below ground, hot rocks heat liquid water higher than boiling point, but trap it so it cannot turn to steam.

AMAZING DISCOVERY

Scientist: James Thomson
Discovery: Triple point of water
Date: 1873
The story: Thomson was an engineer specializing in water transport. He showed that pure water can coexist as a solid, liquid, and water vapor at a particular pressure and temperature: 0.01°C (32.01°F).

Solid Materials

Most objects are made of solid matter. The atoms or molecules that make up a solid are held together very strongly. There are lots of very different solids, but they all share certain features.

Solid Properties

In some solids, the atoms form regular patterns called crystals. Quartz and salt have a crystal structure. In other solids—for example, polythene—the atoms bond in more of a jumble. Some of these shapeless solids can change shape by stretching—this is called being ductile.

A crystal's shape depends on the arrangement of atoms inside. Its hue depends on the elements involved.

The metal iron is ductile. When it's hot, it can be pulled or hammered into shape.

Inside crystals, atoms can be arranged in cubes, hexagons, pyramids, or diamond shapes.

Crystals such as this quartz form by slowly adding new atoms to the outside edges of a growing structure.

Conducting Heat

Solids respond to being heated in different ways. Some solids, including many metals, carry the heat rapidly from one atom to the next. They are called conductors. Others, such as wood or plastic, do not pass on heat. They are called insulators.

In nature, large crystals can can take millions of years to grow. These quartz crystals were grown artificially in just a few hours.

A metal pan conducts heat rapidly through its base to the food inside. However, a wooden spoon (purple and cool in this thermal image) insulates the cook's hand from the heat.

AMAZING DISCOVERY

Scientists: Metalworkers in what is now Turkey
Discovery: Steel
Date: c.2000 BCE
The story: Iron Age metalworkers found that adding other materials to a metal created an alloy that was more useful than the pure metal. For example, people in ancient Turkey found that adding charcoal to iron produced strong steel.

DID YOU KNOW? Tungsten, used in high-performance aircraft, has the highest melting point of any metal. It remains solid up to an amazing 3,414°C (6,277°F).

Liquids and Gases

Most substances are only liquid in a narrow range of temperatures, between their solid and gas phases. Atoms or molecules inside liquids are more loosely bonded than those in solids. In gases, their bonds are even weaker.

Moving Particles

In everyday language, we use "fluid" to mean a liquid. In science, it covers both liquids and gases because their particles can flow more or less freely. Water molecules run very freely but those in treacle are more strongly bonded and flow more slowly. Slow-moving, thick liquids are described as "viscous."

Special photography techniques reveal how the molecules in gases or liquids are constantly moving—for example, in this cough.

Gas Laws

Gases expand to fill the space available. If the gas is contained, its molecules will bounce off the walls of its container, producing pressure. Heating a gas speeds up the movement of its molecules and increases its pressure. Pumping air into a bicycle tyre increases the pressure of gas inside, and also raises its temperature.

In cooler weather, the gas molecules in the tyre slow down. The pressure reduces and the tyre deflates. It has to be pumped up again.

AMAZING DISCOVERY

Scientist: Daniel Bernoulli
Discovery: Bernoulli's principle
Date: 1738
The story: Swiss mathematician Bernoulli discovered that fluids flowing at fast speeds create less pressure than slow-moving ones. The design of an aircraft wing uses this principle to create lift—its shape forces air to move quickly as it passes over its upper surface.

Hot-air balloons work because hot gases rise up through cooler ones. That's because heat moves through fluids by convection—a process where hot parts of the substance expand and flow into colder areas.

The air in the balloon is warmer and lighter than the surrounding cold air, so the balloon floats upward.

The warm air molecules expand and put pressure on the balloon's inner walls so they bulge outward.

DID YOU KNOW? Solid carbon dioxide, or "dry ice," can change straight from being a solid to a gas without passing through a liquid phase at all.

Elements

Elements are the most basic substances. They are made up of tiny identical particles called atoms and they cannot be split into simpler substances. Each element's atoms have unique properties.

Properties, Mixtures, and Compounds

There are 94 elements found in nature. Seventeen are non-metals. They include carbon, oxygen, and nitrogen. Most of the others are metals, apart from six metalloids—elements that sometimes behave like metals and sometimes like non-metals. Two or more elements can mixed together without their atoms bonding. This is a mixture. They can also be combined in a chemical reaction so that their atoms bond. This is a compound.

An element's melting and boiling points decide whether we find it as a solid, liquid, or gas.

Sulfur combines with other elements to form chemical compounds. When it combines with oxygen from the air it forms sulfur dioxide.

This is a mixture of the elements iron and sulfur. Their atoms have not bonded. The iron atoms are magnetic but the sulfur atoms are not. This makes them easy to separate when a magnet is near.

This is iron sulfide, a compound of iron and sulfur. Its atoms cannot be separated without destroying the compound. Iron sulfide is not magnetic, so none of its atoms are attracted to the magnet.

Pure sulfur can have many different forms, depending on the way its atoms bond to form crystals.

DID YOU KNOW? Oxygen is Earth's most common element. Most is locked up in rocks—it accounts for 47 percent of the mass of Earth's crust.

The crater of Ethiopia's Dallol Volcano is covered in sulfur-based chemical compounds, and different forms of pure sulfur.

Atomic Bonds

When atoms bond together, they make larger particles called molecules. The way they bond depends on how many particles called electrons they contain (see page 22). Certain numbers of electrons are more stable than others. Atoms gain or share electrons to reach these stable numbers.

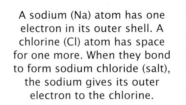

A sodium (Na) atom has one electron in its outer shell. A chlorine (Cl) atom has space for one more. When they bond to form sodium chloride (salt), the sodium gives its outer electron to the chlorine.

When two chlorine (Cl) atoms bond to form a chlorine molecule, they share a pair of electrons. Now each chlorine atom's outer shell has a more stable number of electrons.

AMADING DISCOVERY

Scientist: John Dalton
Discovery: Atomic theory
Date: 1803
The story: Dalton said that all matter is made of atoms, and that atoms are indivisible and indestructible. He observed that all atoms of a given element have the same properties. He also described how compounds are formed by a combination of two or more different kinds of atom.

Periodic Table

The periodic table is a way to display the properties of all 118 elements that have been discovered so far. It lets chemists predict what characteristics an element has just by knowing where it is in the table.

The shape of the periodic table reflects the arrangement of electrons inside atoms. Electrons are the subatomic particles that control chemical reactions between elements.

Periods and Groups

The elements are arranged in seven rows in order of their atomic number—the number of protons that one atom of that element has in its nucleus. Each row is called a period. Elements that share similar properties are arranged in columns called groups. There are 18 groups.

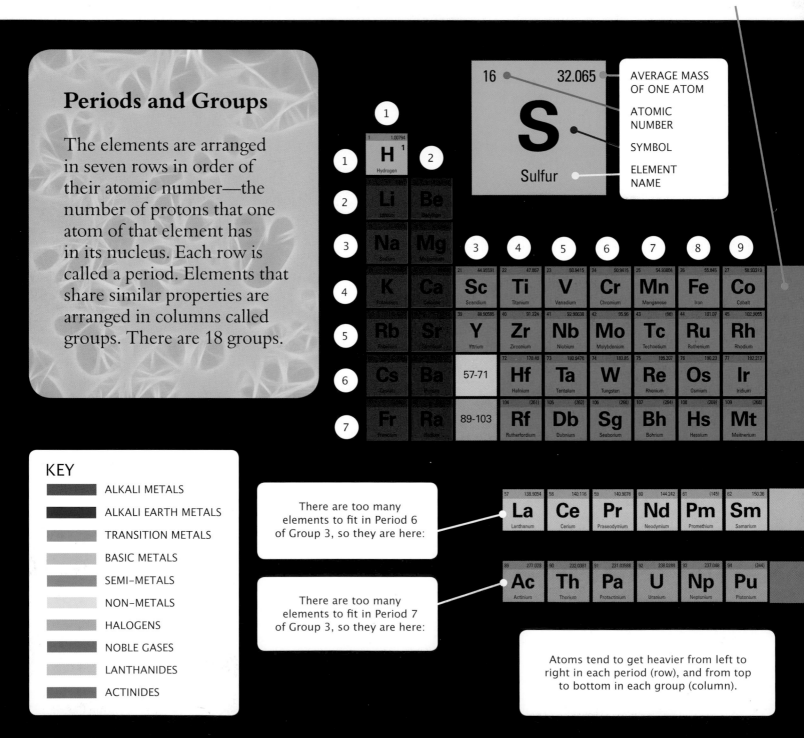

16   32.065

S

Sulfur

AVERAGE MASS OF ONE ATOM

ATOMIC NUMBER

SYMBOL

ELEMENT NAME

KEY

- ALKALI METALS
- ALKALI EARTH METALS
- TRANSITION METALS
- BASIC METALS
- SEMI–METALS
- NON–METALS
- HALOGENS
- NOBLE GASES
- LANTHANIDES
- ACTINIDES

There are too many elements to fit in Period 6 of Group 3, so they are here:

There are too many elements to fit in Period 7 of Group 3, so they are here:

Atoms tend to get heavier from left to right in each period (row), and from top to bottom in each group (column).

Scientist: Dmitri Mendeleev
Discovery: The periodic table
Date: 1869
The story: Mendeleev was one of the first chemists to spot repeating patterns in the chemistry of elements with different masses. This let him to draw up the first periodic table and predict the discovery and properties of new elements.

All the elements in a group have the same number of electrons in their outer shell.

New Elements

Scientists can make new elements in special nuclear reactors. They fire extra particles at the central nuclei of the heaviest elements. More than 20 new elements have been made this way, but they are all unstable and fall apart after just a short time. This is why they are not found in nature.

The elements in Group 18 are called the noble gases and are non-reactive. They all have a full outer shell of electrons.

Physicists build new elements by nuclear fusion— the same process that combines elements inside the Sun.

DID YOU KNOW? Atoms of oganesson, the heaviest element, are so unstable that they disintegrate in less than one-thousandth of a second.

Rocks and Minerals

Most of Earth's elements are naturally locked up in complex chemical molecules. These form solid substances called minerals, which can have beautiful crystal structures. Most rocks are made up from a mix of different minerals. Some elements, such as gold, prefer not to bond with others, so they can be found naturally in pure form.

Elements in the Earth

The rocks that make up Earth's thin outer crust mostly contain just a few fairly light elements. Heavy elements, including precious metals, tend to sink down toward Earth's core. The main elements in the rocky crust are oxygen (47 percent), silicon (28 percent), aluminum (8 percent), iron (5 percent), and calcium (3.5 percent).

Mineral molecules bond together to form crystals. This agate (a form of silicon dioxide) includes crystals on a range of different scales, some too small to see.

Most useful elements are found as chemical compounds in mineral form. Once they have been mined, we use chemical processes to extract the elements.

Gold does not form minerals. These miners are extracting it in its pure form from "veins" in the rock.

Extracting Elements

Minerals that contain useful metals are called ores. They are often in the form of an oxide (the metal has formed a compound with oxygen). If the ore is heated with another chemical, called a reducing agent, there is a chemical reaction that removes the oxygen. This separates out, or extracts, the metal.

Iron is extracted from iron oxide ore by being heated with coke, a form of the element carbon. The coke draws in oxygen and frees the molten iron.

Oxygen is the most plentiful element in Earth's rocks. Minerals based on oxygen are called oxides.

AMAZING DISCOVERY

Scientists: Metalworkers in ancient Mesopotamia (now Iraq)
Discovery: Bronze
Date: c.2800 BCE
The story: Prehistoric people made tools from pure metals found in nature. Metalworkers in the ancient city–state of Ur discovered that combining tin with copper made bronze, an alloy that is harder and stronger than either pure metal.

DID YOU KNOW? Nearly all the rocks and minerals on Earth started out in liquid lava erupted from volcanoes. The only exceptions are meteorites—rocks that fell from space.

17

Chemistry at Work

Chemical reactions rearrange atoms and molecules to create new substances. The substances at the start of a chemical reaction are called reactants. During the reaction their particles break apart, join together, or swap places. They create a new set of substances called products.

How Reactions Work

All chemical reactions take in or give out energy, often in the form of heat, light, or sound. Combustion is an explosive reaction that produces more energy than it takes in. A catalyst is a substance that speeds up a reaction without using energy, and without changing itself.

Combustion is used for fireworks. Gunpowder reacts with oxygen in the air and releases intense heat and bright light. Adding metal salts gives different effects—strontium carbonate produces red fireworks, barium chloride makes green, and calcium chloride creates orange.

Organic Chemistry

The structure of carbon atoms lets them form four strong chemical bonds—the most of any common element. As a result, carbon combines with itself and other atoms to make many different and complex molecules known as organic chemicals. These include the building blocks of life itself.

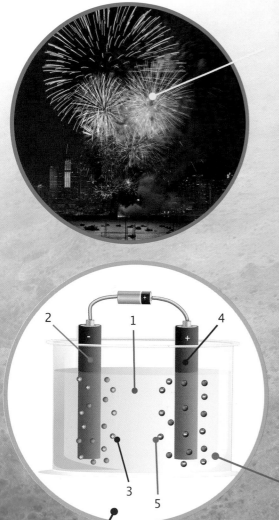

1. Chemicals break apart into positively and negatively charged particles called ions.

2. Negative electrode is a source of electrons.

3. Positive ions combine with electrons to form atoms.

4. Positive electrode draws in electrons.

5. Negative ions give up electrons to form atoms.

Electrolysis uses electrical energy to start a reaction. Electric current is passed through a solution that contains dissolved particles of the reactants.

Seawater is a chemical solution—a mixture of pure water with floating molecules of different chemical compounds.

Chemical reactions are helping to create artificial reefs. The "biorock" forms when a reaction attracts the rocky mineral calcium carbonate to objects—in this case, bikes.

The biorock process is started by electrolysis—passing a small electric current through the seawater.

Corals begin to grow on the build-up of calcium carbonate. Soon other reef creatures will come.

AMAZING DISCOVERY

Scientists: Mikhail Lomonosov, Antoine Lavoisier (left)
Discovery: Balance in reactions
Date: 1748-1774
The story: Chemists Lomonosov and Lavoisier showed that the total mass of substances present before and after a chemical reaction (including any gases released) is the same. This convinced later chemists that reactions involve rearranging fixed numbers of atoms.

DID YOU KNOW? Baking a cake involves chemical reactions. Heat helps the baking powder create bubbles of gas so the cake rises, and it changes the protein in the egg so the cake's firm.

Electrical Properties

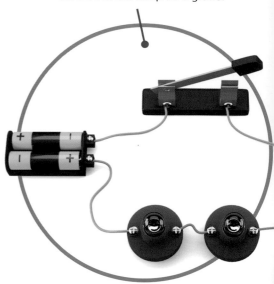

When a switch is closed to complete this circuit, electricity will flow. The current will heat the wire in the lamp so it glows.

Electricity is a form of energy. Every atom has a balance of electric charge in its particles—positive charge in its protons and negative in its electrons. If an atom gains or loses electrons, those charges are no longer balanced. The object becomes electrically charged.

Conductors, Currents, and Circuits

Any electrically charged object has an electromagnetic field around it, which attracts or repels other charged objects. Electricity flows when electrons or other charged particles move. Materials that let electricity flow through them are called electrical conductors. Most metals are good conductors. Charge flowing through a conductor is called an electric current. An electric circuit is a loop of conducting wire that carries current through components with different functions.

A maglev train hovers above the rails, lifted by the repelling force between superconductors and magnets.

The maglev's track is made of very powerful electrical conductors called superconductors.

Maglev is short for "magnetic levitation."

DID YOU KNOW? Electricity from batteries is direct current (DC)—it flows in one direction. Electrical sockets provide alternating current (AC) that changes direction many times a second.

Scientist: Hans–Christian Ørsted
Discovery: Electromagnetic fields
Date: 1820
The story: Danish physicist Ørsted discovered that switching an electric current off and on caused the needle of a nearby magnetic compass to flicker. This was the first evidence that changing currents produce changing magnetic fields around themselves.

Electricity Supply

Electricity from power stations travels along a network of cables. The current travels at high voltages to stop too much power being lost along the way. Devices called transformers step up the voltage as the electricity leaves the power station, and then reduce it to a safe level before it enters our homes, schools, and factories.

Transformers at this electrical substation change high–voltage electricity to suitable lower voltages. Homes need low–voltage electricity, while railways need high voltage.

Coils of conducting wire in the track create an electromagnetic field that pushes the train forward.

Maglev trains like this one in Shanghai can reach speeds of up to 430 km/h (267 mph).

Inside the Atom

Atoms are the building blocks of everyday matter, and the smallest amount of an individual element that can exist. But each atom is made up of even smaller particles. Together, these subatomic particles—protons, neutrons, and electrons—create the atom's overall structure.

Particle Properties

Subatomic particles have particular features. Protons have almost as much mass as a hydrogen atom, and carry a positive electric charge. Neutrons have a similar mass but no electric charge. Electrons have much less mass than the other particles, and carry a negative electric charge equal and opposite to the proton's charge.

This amazing photograph shows tracks left behind by subatomic particles as they move through fluid. Scientists smash atoms together to create subatomic particles (see pages 82–83).

Particles follow different paths depending on their mass and electric charge.

The positive charge of protons (red) in an atom's nucleus is usually balanced by the negative charge of electrons (blue) orbiting around it. The atom's mass comes from a combination of protons and neutrons (white).

The particles leave behind bubbles as they pass through liquid hydrogen.

Quarks

Each proton and neutron is made up of three even smaller subatomic particles called quarks. Quarks are attracted together by the extremely powerful strong nuclear force (see page 83). This overcomes the electromagnetic force that pushes positively charged protons away from each other, and explains why the nuclei of atoms do not just fly apart.

There are six kinds of quark. "Up" quarks are the lightest and "down" quarks are the second-lightest. Protons have two up quarks and a down quark. Neutrons have two down quarks and an up quark.

AMAZING DISCOVERY

Scientists: Ernest Rutherford, Hans Geiger, Ernest Marsden
Discovery: The atomic nucleus
Date: 1911
The story: Rutherford's team fired particles into a thin sheet of gold. Most passed straight through, but a few bounced back. This revealed that the gold atoms were mostly empty space, with mass concentrated in a tiny nucleus.

DID YOU KNOW? If an atom of hydrogen (the simplest element) was blown up to the size of a football stadium, its central nucleus would be no larger than a pea!

Quantum World

Matter on everyday scales tends to behave in easily predictable ways. We need a very different set of rules, called quantum physics, to describe matter on the very smallest scales and help us guess how atoms and subatomic particles will behave.

Waves or Particles?

The key to quantum physics is a strange idea called wave-particle duality. Very small particles sometimes behave like waves, and we can't measure all their properties accurately at the same time. So if we measure a particle's speed we can't pin down its position, and if we pin down its position we lose track of its speed.

Quantum physics lies behind the electron microscope, which lets us view tiny creatures in huge detail.

Electron microscope images of bugs, ticks, fleas, and other small creatures can magnify details by up to two million times.

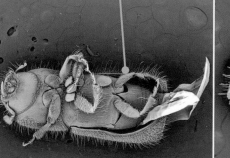

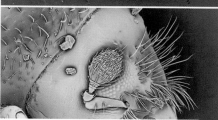

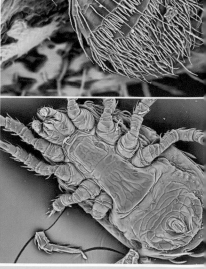

An atom can be viewed as a particle or a wave. The smallest particles (top) have relatively long wavelengths. Larger ones (bottom) have much shorter wavelengths.

DID YOU KNOW? An electron wave has a wavelength 300–500 times smaller than a light wave.

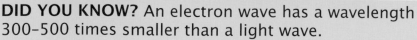

Scientists: Louis de Broglie, Erwin Schrödinger (left)
Discovery: Wave–particle duality
Date: 1924–1926
The story: In 1924, de Broglie suggested that just as light waves can also act like particles, perhaps small particles could behave like waves. Two years later, Schrödinger worked out an equation for describing these waves.

Quantum Physics and the Everyday World

There are lots of uncertainties in quantum physics, but it also answers questions ranging from how stars shine to how plants make energy from sunlight. Many technologies rely on our understanding that subatomic particles can also behave as waves, including nuclear power, solar panels, modern electronics, and lasers.

Electrons have much shorter wavelengths than light waves, so they can pick out finer detail.

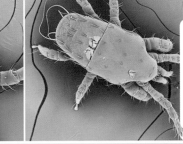

Lasers are intense beams of light. They are produced by pumping atoms full of electrical energy so that they produce rapid bursts of photons (light waves).

Kingdoms of Life

Our planet is home to nearly nine million species (types of living thing). They range from tiny bacteria to blue whales and from humans to giant redwood trees. Biologists group together species that share characteristics to create a complex "tree of life." They organize living things into five kingdoms: animals, plants, fungi, prokaryotes (bacteria and blue-green algae), and protoctists (such as amoebas).

Bacteria use chemical reactions and cell division to survive and copy themselves. The first living organism did this too.

One Big Family

All living things are descended from a single common ancestor—a simple organism that lived about four billion years ago. This organism's descendants found different ways to survive. They branched out to produce the millions of species on Earth today, as well as countless others along the way.

What is a Species?

Living things belong in the same species if they can breed with each other and produce offspring that can also breed. It's not always possible to test this, but scientists can look for shared genes or body features instead.

Dogs come in an amazing variety of shapes and sizes, but they are a single species. Because their genes are almost identical, different breeds can mate and have puppies.

Coral reefs, like this one off the island of Fiji in the South Pacific, are home to tens of thousands of species.

AMAZING DISCOVERY

Scientist: Carl Linnaeus
Discovery: The tree of life
Date: 1735
The story: Swedish scientist Linnaeus invented a two–name system for classifying every living thing by its genus and species (e.g. *Homo sapiens* for modern humans). This was the first step toward grouping species in a tree of life.

Scientists collect each group of closely related species together into a genus. Related genera are grouped into families, families into orders, orders into classes, classes into phyla, and phyla into kingdoms.

Three–quarters of all living organisms are found on land.

The green sea turtle, *Chelonia mydas*, belongs to a larger family of sea turtles called the Cheloniidae.

DID YOU KNOW? Scientists estimate that about 99 percent of all the species that have ever lived are now extinct.

Story of DNA

Every living thing has its own set of instructions that tells it how to create the chemicals vital to life—and how to put them together. These instructions, called genes, are found inside a long, twisty molecule called DNA (short for deoxyribonucleic acid).

Pairs and Patterns

The DNA molecule looks like a spiral ladder. The ladder's "rungs" are made of pairs of chemicals called bases. The order of the base pairs spells out a code that can be used to build proteins and other chemicals.

The DNA molecule forms a long, winding ladder shape that is called a double helix.

ADENINE

THYMINE

GUANINE

CYTOSINE

BASE PAIR

The ladder rungs are made of pairs of chemicals—either adenine and thyamine or guanine and cytosine.

DID YOU KNOW? The longest human chromosome, known as chromosome 1, contains more than 249 million base pairs.

DNA is coiled into structures called chromosomes. We have 46 chromosomes (23 pairs) in each cell (except for sperm and egg cells, which have 23 unpaired chromosomes).

Sections of DNA can "unzip" down the middle. When this happens, each half can be used to build a new, identical molecule.

Inherited Instructions

Each human cell contains 23 chromosomes from the father and 23 from the mother. These carry thousands of genes for different functions. Every time a cell divides to become two new cells, all 46 chromosomes are copied too.

Chromosomes look X–shaped during cell division because they have copied themselves into two strands.

Each rung in the DNA ladder is made of two interlocked bases or chemicals.

AMAZING DISCOVERY

Scientists: Francis Crick, James Watson, Rosalind Franklin, Maurice Wilkins
Discovery: The double helix structure of DNA
Date: 1953
The story: Crick and Watson worked out the shape of the DNA molecule based on measurements taken by Franklin and Wilkins. The three men were awarded the Nobel Prize in 1962.

Cell Machinery

All living organisms are made up of tiny building blocks called cells. Most cells are microscopic, but they are very complicated. They can convert food into energy, make useful chemicals, and reproduce themselves. The simplest life forms are just one cell; the most complex contain millions.

Two Types of Cell

There are two main types of cell. Bacteria and single-celled organisms have prokaryotic cells—simple cells that do not have a separate nucleus to contain their DNA. Larger organisms have eukaryotic cells. These contain separate chemical machines called organelles that carry out different functions.

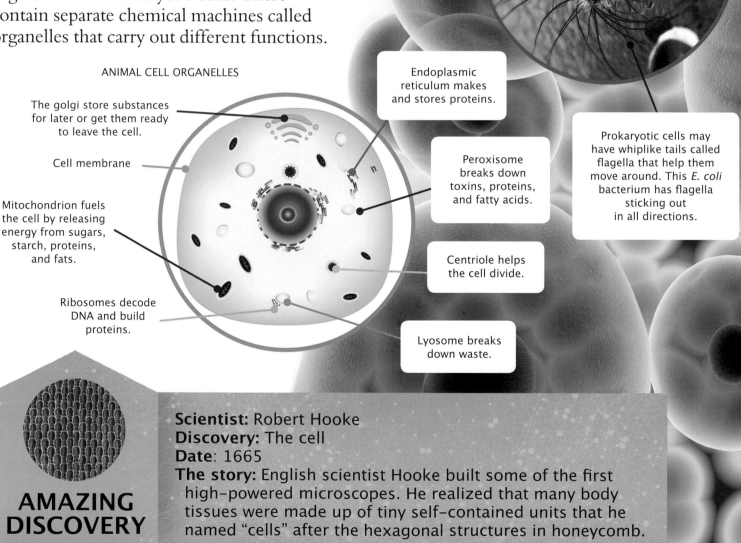

ANIMAL CELL ORGANELLES

The golgi store substances for later or get them ready to leave the cell.

Cell membrane

Mitochondrion fuels the cell by releasing energy from sugars, starch, proteins, and fats.

Ribosomes decode DNA and build proteins.

Endoplasmic reticulum makes and stores proteins.

Peroxisome breaks down toxins, proteins, and fatty acids.

Centriole helps the cell divide.

Lyosome breaks down waste.

Prokaryotic cells may have whiplike tails called flagella that help them move around. This *E. coli* bacterium has flagella sticking out in all directions.

AMAZING DISCOVERY

Scientist: Robert Hooke
Discovery: The cell
Date: 1665
The story: English scientist Hooke built some of the first high-powered microscopes. He realized that many body tissues were made up of tiny self-contained units that he named "cells" after the hexagonal structures in honeycomb.

In all eukaryotic cells the nucleus holds most of the genetic material, or DNA.

Making Copies

Cells can reproduce in one of two ways. Mitosis is a process that creates perfect copies. It is used during body growth and to replace damaged or dead cells. Meiosis creates special cells with 23 unpaired chromosomes. The process of meiosis creates our reproductive cells (sperm in males or eggs in females).

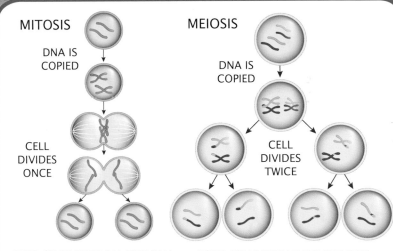

MITOSIS

DNA IS COPIED

CELL DIVIDES ONCE

TWO CELLS WITH ALL THE DNA (46 CHROMOSOMES)

MEIOSIS

DNA IS COPIED

CELL DIVIDES TWICE

FOUR CELLS WITH HALF THE DNA (23 CHROMOSOMES)

Mitosis creates two copies of the cell's DNA, then the cell splits to create two exact copies. In meiosis, two copies of the DNA are also made, but the cell divides twice to produce four cells that each contain half the original amount of DNA.

Cell walls let substances in and out. In animal cells like this, the wall is a thin membrane. Plant cell walls are thicker and more rigid.

A jellylike fluid called cytoplasm is inside the cell. The organelles float in it.

DID YOU KNOW? Animal cells are usually between 0.001 mm (0.00004 in) and 0.1 mm (0.004 in) in size.

31

Plants

There are nearly 400,000 plant species on Earth. Plants are living things that can make their own food. During this process they produce oxygen, the gas that all animals, including humans, must breathe to stay alive.

Food from Sunlight

Plants take in carbon dioxide from the air through their leaves and water from the soil through their roots. Then they use the energy in sunlight to transform these ingredients into sugars. This process, called photosynthesis, is a chemical reaction. It takes place in the leaves, helped by a green chemical called chlorophyll.

This cross-section of a leaf shows the transport vessels in the middle. These carry water to the leaf and sugary glucose away from it.

Plant Reproduction

Seedless plants, such as liverworts, mosses, and ferns, reproduce by releasing spores. If a spore lands in a suitable place, it produces sex cells and, after fertilization, a new plant can grow. Seed plants produce seeds when male sex cells fertilize female ones. A seed contains a complete embryo plant along with a supply of food.

Pollen contains male sex cells. These must reach other flowers to fertilize their female sex cells. Pollen can be carried by insects and birds that visit the flower to feed on nectar.

Tree trunks are made of cellulose, the tough, fibrous material that forms plants' cell walls.

To get as much light as possible, plants hold themselves upright using a stem or trunk.

Like all conifers, the sequoia makes its seeds on special scales that are packed together to form cones.

Roots below the ground anchor plants so they don't fall over. They also suck up water and nutrients from the soil.

AMAZING DISCOVERY

Scientist: Jan Ingenhousz
Discovery: Photosynthesis
Date: 1779
The story: This Dutch scientist discovered that plants release different gases if kept in sunlight or darkness. He realized that they absorb carbon dioxide from the atmosphere to build their bodies.

DID YOU KNOW? Some plants grow at amazing speeds. Bamboo can shoot up by as much as 91 cm (35 in) in a single day.

Animals

Animals are living things that get their energy from food, water, oxygen, and the Sun. Unlike plants, they can usually move around in search of food. To harvest energy from their food, animals need to breathe in oxygen.

Animal Types

Fish, amphibians, reptiles, birds, and mammals all have a backbone and skeleton to support their body. They are called vertebrates and make up less than 10 percent of animals. The rest are invertebrates, which don't have a skeleton. They include arthropods, such as insects and spiders, which have a tough outer casing called an exoskeleton, and soft-bodied mollusks.

Symmetry

Most animals have a body plan that is symmetrical—the same on both sides. Features such as limbs and some organs are copied in mirror image. The gut, used to process food, leads from one end of the body to the other.

Centipedes and millipedes

Spiders

Insects

ARTHROPODS

Crustaceans

Annelids

Mollusks

Roundworms

PSEUDOCOELOMATES

ACOELOMATES

Flatworms

Sponges

Symmetry appears in the very first few cells of a developing animal embryo. It often appears in adult features, such as this tiger's beautiful fur.

AMAZING DISCOVERY

Scientist: Jennifer Clack
Discovery: *Acanthostega*
Date: 1987
The story: When Clack found a skeleton of *Acanthostega* in Greenland—"Boris"—she realized it was a key step in the evolution of tetrapods (land vertebrates). Boris lived 360 million years ago and had a fishlike body with four legs. She later found tracks of another early tetrapod.

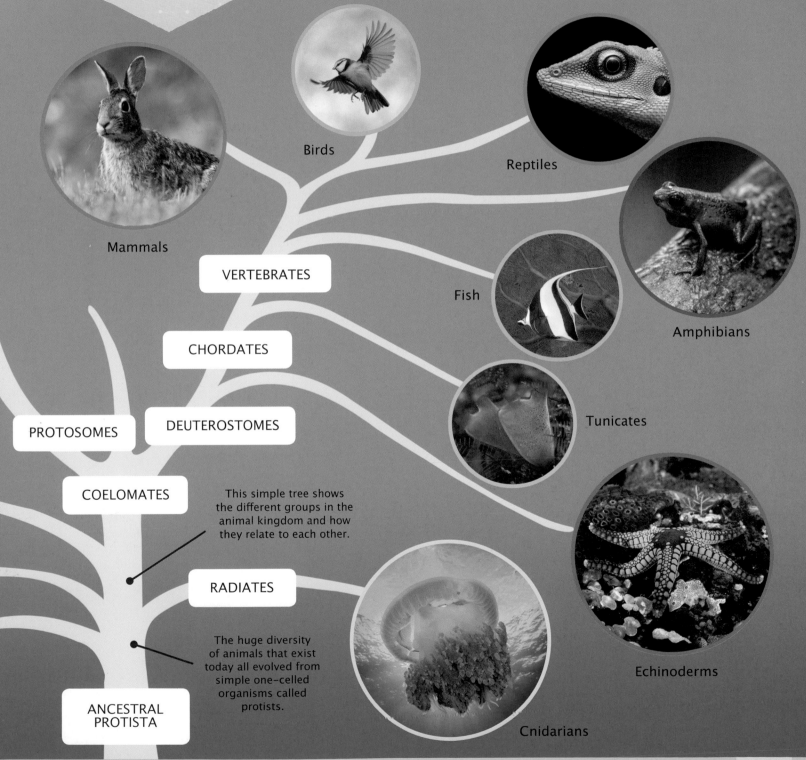

Birds

Reptiles

Mammals

VERTEBRATES

Fish

Amphibians

CHORDATES

Tunicates

PROTOSOMES

DEUTEROSTOMES

COELOMATES

This simple tree shows the different groups in the animal kingdom and how they relate to each other.

RADIATES

The huge diversity of animals that exist today all evolved from simple one-celled organisms called protists.

Echinoderms

ANCESTRAL PROTISTA

Cnidarians

DID YOU KNOW? Arthropods account for 80 percent of all known animal species. Most are small, but the Japanese spider crab has a legspan up to 5.5 m (18 ft).

Web of Life

Living things are connected and dependent on each other through a complex web of relationships known as an ecosystem. These relationships keep the numbers of different species in balance. Species can come under threat if anything upsets this balance, such as changes to the environment.

Everything is Connected

Plants generate the oxygen that animals need. They are also food for plant-eating animals (herbivores). In turn, meat-eating animals (carnivores) hunt herbivores. All living animals release the carbon dioxide that plants need for photosynthesis. When a plant or animal dies, bacteria, fungi, and other organisms help to recycle its nutrients back into the soil.

The way living things depend on each other for food is called a food chain. A predator such as a big cat is right at the top of the food chain, because no other animal hunts it.

Plants are called producers because they make their own food. Animals are called consumers because they eat plants and other animals.

Mushrooms are fungi. There are around 5.1 million species of fungus.

AMAZING DISCOVERY

Scientists: James Lovelock, Lynn Margulis
Discovery: Gaia theory
Date: 1972–1979
The story: Chemist Lovelock and microbiologist Margulis showed how living things can affect Earth's atmosphere, oceans, and even rocks. Their Gaia theory argues that our entire planet is a single vast ecosystem.

A tree can be a home to mosses, ivy, and other plants, as well as providing animals with food, oxygen, and shelter.

Most of the fungus is made up of underground threads called hyphae. They feed on nutrients in the soil.

Introduced Species

Within any ecosystem, numbers of different species may go up and down, but they usually return to a balance point. If a new species is introduced into an ecosystem, however, it can have a devastating effect. It competes with the existing species for food, water, space, and breeding sites—and it might spread disease too.

Away from its native Amazon basin and the bugs that feed on it there, the water hyacinth is an invader. It is fast-growing and crowds out other aquatic plants.

DID YOU KNOW? The dodo, a giant flightless bird from Mauritius, died out within 80 years of humans and their rats, pigs, dogs, and cats landing on its island home.

Extremes of Life

Most living things need a habitat that offers clean air, a reasonable temperature, and water that is not too acidic or salty. However, some organisms manage to thrive in extreme conditions that would kill most living things.

Coping with Anything

Living things that do well in deadly environments are called extremophiles. Most are single-celled microorganisms. They survive because they have evolved internal chemical processes that stop them being damaged by very high or low temperatures, excess acid or salt, or other difficulties. Many extremophiles can even draw energy from their hostile surroundings.

In the deepest parts of the ocean, volcanic vents pump out scorching, sulfur-rich water. Extremophile microbes survive there and provide the base for an ecosystem that includes deep-sea jellyfish.

Water in Yellowstone Park's hot springs can be 93°C (199°F).

Yellowstone's Grand Prismatic Spring is named for the red, yellow, and green extremophile microbes around its edges.

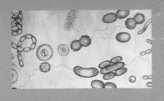

AMAZING DISCOVERY

Scientist: Carl Woese
Discovery: Extreme microbes
Date: 1977
The story: In the mid–1970s, explorers found life thriving in apparently hostile conditions around deep-sea volcanic vents. Woese discovered that these complex ecosystems are based on an entirely new type of single-celled organism, now called archaea.

The orange comes from carotenoids, which the microbes use to carry out photosynthesis.

Hardy Tardigrades

Tardigrades, also known as water bears, are some of the most amazing animals known to science. They usually live among mosses and lichens. However, they can withstand high doses of radiation, extreme hot and cold, dehydration, high pressures, and even exposure to the vacuum of space.

Tardigrades are eight-legged invertebrates probably related to arthropods and velvet worms. They were only discovered in 1773, but have since been found in a huge range of environments.

DID YOU KNOW? Life may have evolved around deep-sea vents before adapting to other conditions. If so, land-living animals and plants are the real extremophiles!

Darwin's Theory

Why are some species of living thing so similar to each other, and others so different? Does one species change or evolve into another over time? These questions puzzled scientists for centuries—until British naturalist Charles Darwin came up with his theory of evolution by natural selection.

Darwin was inspired by the many new species that explorers were discovering. He also wanted to explain the existence of fossils that were many millions of years old.

Voyage of the *Beagle*

Darwin's theory was driven by his studies aboard the survey ship HMS *Beagle* in the 1830s. In Patagonia he found fossils of giant extinct mammals, such as *Megatherium*. Visiting the isolated Galápagos Islands, Darwin observed finches, marine iguanas, and tortoises that had adapted to different island homes.

Darwin's Finches

There are about 15 finch species across the Galápagos, and they show evolution in action. A single ancestor species became stranded on the volcanic islands some time after their formation. Over time, their descendents spread across the islands and their beaks adapted to suit the main food on each island.

John Gould, the *Beagle*'s natural history artist, sketched the finches in the Galápagos. Their beaks had evolved to suit particular foods. Nut-eaters had large, short bills for cracking shells. Insect-catchers had longer, pointier bills.

This is one of five giant tortoise species on Isabela Island, the most recently formed of the Galápagos Islands.

Each species has a unique shell shape. The tortoises also come in a range of sizes.

Giant tortoises live on seven of the Galápagos Islands. There are more than ten different species.

AMAZING DISCOVERY

Scientists: Charles Darwin (left), Alfred Russel Wallace
Discovery: The origin of the species
Date: 1859
The story: Darwin spent 20 years after the *Beagle* developing his ideas about evolution and natural selection. He published his theory only receiving a letter from Wallace, who had come up with a similar theory while exploring South America and Asia.

DID YOU KNOW? French scientist Jean–Baptiste Lamarck was the first to suggest species arise through a process of evolution in 1800—but he couldn't explain how.

Evolution at Work

Each year, vast herds of wildebeest and zebra migrate across the Serengeti to better grazing. Only the fittest survive.

Evolution explains how living things slowly change over many generations and new species arise. Each individual has a slightly different mix of genetic instructions from its parents. Genes that give it a better chance of survival are more likely to be passed on to the next generation. Over time, individuals with a particular advantage outbreed and replace those without it.

Selection Pressures

Natural selection drives evolution. It's about how individuals adapt to different pressures from the environment. These can include availability of food, competition for mates, threats from predators, diseases, or a changing climate. The fittest usually survive and breed, passing on the genes that helped them cope with the conditions.

Megatherium was a giant ground sloth that died out 10,000 years ago. It could not face the selection pressure from changes in its habitat. Today the only sloths are small tree-dwellers.

The journey is tough. It weeds out any individuals that tire easily or are prone to disease.

The most dangerous moment of the migration is when the animals must cross the crocodile-infested Mara river.

Scientist: J. W. Tutt
Discovery: Evolution in the peppered moth
Date: 1896
The story: Tutt suggested that peppered moths had grown darker during the Industrial Revolution. Darker moths were less likely to be spotted and eaten by birds in a polluted, sooty environment, so more of them survived to reproduce.

Crocodiles have evolved to survive for up to a year without food—and then feast.

Evolution and Genes

Although Darwin came up with the theory of evolution, he had no idea how parents passed on adaptations to their offspring. Today we know that evolution works because characteristics are inherited from a mix of both parents' genes, with a little random mutation (due to errors in copying DNA) thrown in.

Austrian monk Gregor Mendel was the first person to identify what we call genes. He noticed them through breeding pea plants with different characteristics. This was in the 1860s, but Mendel's important work was overlooked for decades.

DID YOU KNOW? Biologists study evolution at high speed using the *Drosophila* fruit fly—a species that can produce a new generation every ten days!

History of Life

Life has existed on Earth for about four billion years. For most of that time, known as the Precambrian, it was just simple, single-celled organisms. From around 540 million years ago (mya), there has been more complex life, and it has passed through distinct phases.

Divisions of Time

The story of complex life on Earth is usually broken into three stages—the Paleozoic, Mesozoic, and Cenozoic eras (meaning ancient, middle, and recent life). Each era is divided into geological periods lasting tens of millions of years. Geologists identify these periods from the types of rock and the presence of particular fossils.

Fossils of trilobites only come from the six periods that form the Paleozoic. They appeared in the first of these periods, the Cambrian, and went extinct in the last, the Permian.

Anomalocaris was an ancestor of arthropods. It lived in the oceans 510 mya, during the Cambrian period.

Mass Extinctions

Throughout history, major changes in life on Earth have begun with natural disasters such as impacts from space, volcanic eruptions, or climate change. These disasters wipe out many of the previously dominant animals, leaving the way open for new ones to take their place.

About 65 mya, the effects of a huge asteroid impact drove the dinosaurs to extinction. Since then, mammals have become the main large land animals.

Flowering plants appeared 145 mya, in the Cretaceous, the last period of the Mesozoic.

The Mesozoic was the age of reptiles. Dinosaurs dominated the land, and their cousins ruled the air and seas.

Many human (*Homo*) species evolved and died out during the Pleistocene. Only ours, *Homo sapiens*, survives.

The Paleozoic saw most modern groups of animals evolve and life move from the water onto the land.

Dimetrodon was a synapsid, a mammal–like reptile that lived in the Permian period, before the dinosaurs.

Smilodon appeared at the start of the Quarternary period, 2.5 mya. It died out at the end of the last Ice Age.

AMAZING DISCOVERY

Scientists: Jack Sepkoski, David Raup
Discovery: Mass extinctions
Date: 1982
The story: Raup and Sepkoski identified five major extinctions in the history of complex life on Earth. A couple of years later, scientists linked the most recent extinction, 65 mya, to an asteroid crashing into Earth.

DID YOU KNOW? Birds evolved from dinosaurs called theropods. They survived the mass extinction 65 mya, but the other dinosaurs did not.

Amazing Body

The body is a complex collection of about 37 trillion cells that work together to create a living, thinking human being. Those cells are joined together to make tissues that have different properties. The tissues build up into organs with specific jobs, from pumping blood to making hormones.

Body Systems

The body has systems to look after different functions. Bones and muscles provide support and movement. The brain and nerves gather information about our surroundings and help us to respond. The heart and lungs provide muscles with fuel. The digestive system harvests energy from the food we eat. Other systems repair the body and keep it stable.

OTHER ELEMENTS

NITROGEN

HYDROGEN

CARBON

OXYGEN

Some body systems involve an organ in a particular place, such as the lungs. Others, such as the nervous system, are spread throughout our body.

Human Recipe

We are built from common chemical elements. Oxygen makes up 65 percent of our mass, 9.5 percent is lightweight hydrogen, and 18.5 percent is carbon (a versatile element that builds the complex chemicals necessary for life). Nitrogen, calcium, and phosphorus account for 5.2 percent. The remaining 1.8 percent is made up of tiny amounts of other elements.

Most of our body's oxygen and hydrogen is locked up in water molecules (H_2O). Water makes up 55–60 percent of an adult's body weight, and more in children.

Scientist: Andreas Vesalius
Discovery: Human anatomy
Date: 1543
The story: Brussels–born physician Vesalius pioneered the dissection of dead human bodies. He made countless discoveries and overturned mistaken ideas about human anatomy that doctors had stuck to for almost 1,400 years.

The systems of the body are always working, whether the body is at rest or doing something energetic.

The brain tells the body what to do based on information gathered by the eyes, ears, and other sensory organs.

The digestive system provides the energy to run. It gathers nutrients from food, which the blood carries to every cell.

Bones support the legs, and muscles make it possible for them to move. The directions that make the legs run come from the brain.

DID YOU KNOW? Most body cells can only be seen through a microscope, but an egg cell is just visible with the naked eye at 0.1 mm (0.004 in) across.

Inside the Brain

The human brain is the most complex structure in all of nature. It is packed with 86 billion individual cells called neurons, which form a vast web of connections. These neurons send signals with little bursts of electric charge that are carried by a flow of chemicals washing around the brain.

How the Brain Works

Our brain is split into different regions, each made up of neurons that are specialized to carry out particular tasks. Areas near the middle and bottom of the brain handle instinctive tasks and help regulate our body. The wrinkly outer layer of the brain, called the cerebral cortex, is in charge of more complex tasks such as thinking and sensory processing.

The cerebral cortex's wrinkles give neurons maximum space. The wrinklier the brain, the more processing it can do!

On each side of the cerebral cortex there are four distinct areas called lobes.

The frontal lobes look after emotions, thinking, memory, planning, language, and more.

The parietal lobes are concerned with the senses of taste and touch.

The occipital lobes are where we process information from our eyes.

The temporal lobes manage our hearing.

AMANING DISCOVERY

Scientist: Santiago Ramón y Cajal
Discovery: The neuron doctrine
Date: 1888
The story: Spanish anatomist Ramón y Cajal used new techniques to study neurons under the microscope. He showed that the nervous system was made up of individual nerve cells that formed temporary connections when they were passing on chemical instructions.

The corpus callosum connects the left and right halves of the brain.

Scanning the Brain

Scientists study living, thinking brains with machines that map where electric charge is flowing at a particular time. Even the most advanced scanners cannot yet see specific neurons "firing." However, they can see enough to show that complex thinking involves networks of neurons spread across the cortex, rather than small, specific areas.

The cerebellum at the back controls movement and balance.

The brain stem is in charge of "automatic" functions such as breathing and heart rate.

A magnetic resonance imaging (MRI) scanner briefly exposes the brain to a magnetic field. It records how magnetized atoms in different parts of the brain absorb and emit radio waves.

SPINAL CORD

Bone and Muscle

Bones are a special type of rigid, hardened tissue that supports the weight of the human body and gives it an overall shape. Cartilage is a tough but flexible connective tissue that holds the framework of bones together. Muscles attached to bones can pull in different directions so our body changes shape and can move.

Our Skeleton

Babies are born with 300 bones in their body, but as we grow some of these join together—most adults have 206. Bones get their toughness from a mineral called calcium phosphate. Despite their solid appearance, bones are spongy inside, and filled with a tissue called marrow that produces the body's blood cells.

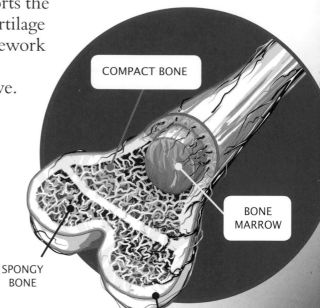

COMPACT BONE

BONE MARROW

SPONGY BONE

Most of our blood cells are manufactured by bone marrow in the large, ball-like ends of long bones such as the femur or hip bone.

Muscle Tissues

Muscles are made up of special cells that can reduce in length, creating a pulling force. Skeletal muscle is the most common type, made up of stringy bundles. Smooth muscle lines blood vessels and various body organs. Cardiac muscle is a special kind of muscle in the heart that can work without resting.

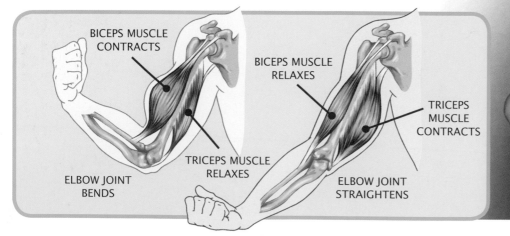

BICEPS MUSCLE CONTRACTS

BICEPS MUSCLE RELAXES

TRICEPS MUSCLE CONTRACTS

TRICEPS MUSCLE RELAXES

ELBOW JOINT BENDS

ELBOW JOINT STRAIGHTENS

Together, the feet contain 52 bones— that's one-quarter of all the bones in the body.

Muscles can only pull, not push, so many skeletal muscles work together in opposing pairs. As one relaxes and the other contracts, they make a joint move.

The elbow joint is where the humerus bone in the upper arm meets the ulna and radius bones in the lower arm.

The skull is made up of 22 bones. The cranium, which protects the brain, has eight bones, while 14 bones form the face.

Each finger is made up of three bones called phalanges. The thumb has two phalanges.

The pelvis includes the hip bones and pubic bone. It protects internal organs and also lets the body move.

AMAZING DISCOVERY

Scientist: Luigi Galvani
Discovery: Electric muscles
Date: 1786
The story: Italian physician Galvani found that muscles in the legs of a dissected frog twitched when he touched them with wires from a battery. Today, electric charge is used in emergencies to restart the heart muscles.

DID YOU KNOW? The largest bone in the human body is the femur (thigh bone). The smallest is the stapes in the middle ear, which is just 3 mm (0.12 in) long.

Nervous System

The brain and spinal cord make up the central nervous system. They contain neurons—specialized nerve cells that carry information around the brain, and between the brain and body. There are two other kinds of nerve cell—sensory nerves and motor nerves—which look after our senses and movement.

Signals and Synapses

Information travels from neuron to neuron as bursts of electrically charged chemicals. Signals cross tiny gaps between the neurons, called synapses, and enter the next neuron through one of its short tendrils, called dendrites. Signals leave the neuron along its one extra-long tendril, the axon, and cross synapses into other neurons.

On Two Levels

Part of the nervous system works automatically without us having to think about it. It controls organs and body functions, and sends signals to relax the body or prepare it for action. The other part of the nervous system handles tasks that require more complex thought, such as interpreting senses and moving muscles.

The spinal cord is the highway between the body and the brain. Nerves branch off it to every part of the body.

When it is tapped by the doctor's hammer, the knee jerks involuntarily. This is a reflex action. Nearby nerve cells make the knee jerk without waiting for directions from the brain. Reflexes help to protect the body from harm.

The axon is like a long, very thin wire. It carries outgoing electrical signals from the neuron.

Dendrites receive incoming electrical signals from other neurons.

Branching off the neuron's body are many small tendrils, called dendrites, and one long one, called the axon.

The cell body contains the nucleus, which houses the cell's DNA.

AMAZING DISCOVERY

Scientists: Andrew Huxley, Alan Hodgkin, John Eccles
Discovery: The nature of nerve signals
Date: 1963
The story: Experiments using squid nerve cells (the longest known) let these biologists trace the movement of signals from one end to another. They revealed how a wave of rapid chemical changes transports electric charge.

DID YOU KNOW? The longest nerve cell in the human body is the sciatic nerve. It runs from the lower back all the way down to the big toe.

Skin and Hair

Just like the heart or liver, the skin is an organ—a part of the body with a particular job. Its layers have nerves, hairs, and glands that protect the body's delicate inner tissues, keep its temperature steady, and let us touch.

Skin Structure

The skin has three layers. The outer epidermis is made of cells with no blood supply, and creates a waterproof barrier. The middle dermis has a rich blood supply and many sense receptors. The inner hypodermis lies directly over muscles, bones, and organs. It stores the body's fuel reserves in the form of fat.

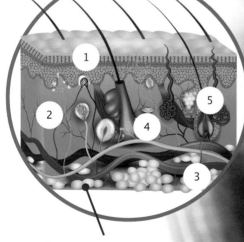

This cross-section of the skin shows its three layers: the epidermis (1), dermis (2), and hypodermis (3). The dermis contains hair follicles (4) and sense receptors (5).

Every follicle contains two pigments. The exact mix decides how dark or light the hair is.

Hairs are thin shafts of a protein called keratin. They grow out of roots called follicles in the dermis layer of the skin.

As we age, the skin becomes less elastic. It develops lines and wrinkles.

Hair

Compared to most mammals humans have very little hair, but it still does important jobs. Head hair protects us from sunburn and losing body heat. Eyebrows, eyelashes, and nose and ear hairs stop microbes, dust, and parasites entering the body. Some hairs help with our sense of touch too.

In the epidermis, older skin cells push closer to the surface. They flatten, dry out, and eventually flake off.

Hair and skin keep our temperature steady. Hairs help sweat evaporate off our skin and cool us down. They can also stand on end to trap a layer of air close to the skin that warms us up.

AMAZING DISCOVERY

Scientist: Ibn Sina (Avicenna)
Discovery: Skin creams
Date: 1025
The story: Persian philosopher Ibn Sina wrote about skin conditions in his medical handbook of 1025. He recommended the use of zinc oxide, a chemical compound that is still used today to soothe rashes.

Digestive System

Like all animals, humans need to harvest energy from food to survive. This process is called digestion. A series of organs, linked to one another along a tube called the gastrointestinal tract (gut), break down the food, remove its useful nutrients, and get rid of any waste.

The liver produces bile that helps to digest fats and remove cholesterol and other waste products.

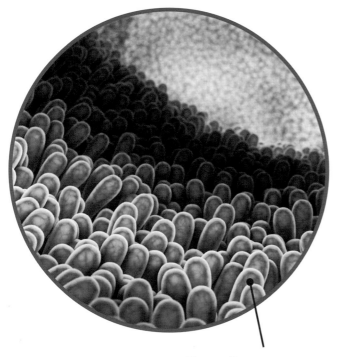

The small intestine is lined with thousands of tiny protrusions called villi. Digested nutrients pass through their thin walls and into the bloodstream.

In and Out

When we swallow, chewed-up food squeezes down a tube called the gullet or esophagus to the stomach. Here, strong muscles mush up the food and gastric juices begin to break it down. The intestines absorb the nutrients from the food into the bloodstream, leaving behind waste that is pushed out of the rectum.

The large intestine processes the watery waste that leaves the small intestine. It absorbs water back into the bloodstream and creates solid waste—poop.

AMANZING DISCOVERY

Scientist: Jan Baptiste van Helmont
Discovery: Chemical digestion
Date: 1662
The story: Van Helmont argued against a popular idea that heat was responsible for breaking down food in the stomach. He argued that digestion is mostly done by chemical agents—what modern scientists call enzymes.

DID YOU KNOW? The small intestine is about 6 m (20 ft) long. The large intestine is only about 1.5 m (5 ft) long, but is much wider.

The stomach contains gastric juices—highly acidic liquid full of enzymes that break down the chemicals in food.

Cleansing Kidneys

The kidneys get rid of any waste chemicals created by our own organs. They contain about a million tiny tubes called nephrons that filter salts and other waste from the bloodstream. The liquid left behind—urine—passes down tubes called ureters to the bladder. The kidneys process up to 200 l (44 gallons) of blood every day.

The pancreas produces enzymes that help to break down carbohydrates, proteins, and fats. It also keeps blood sugar levels steady.

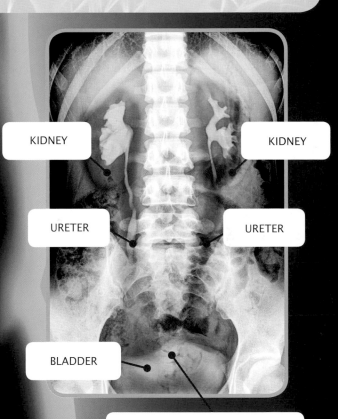

KIDNEY

KIDNEY

URETER

URETER

BLADDER

Once the bladder is about half full, nerve signals warn the brain that it needs to be emptied. We urinate (pee) by relaxing the urethra muscle at the base of the bladder.

The small intestine is where most digestion happens, and most of the nutrients are absorbed.

In the small intestine, the food is reduced to simple sugars, fats, and proteins. These pass into the blood.

Heart, Blood, and Lungs

Blood is the body's transport system. It moves many different chemicals and other materials around our body, pumped by a powerful muscle, the heart. The blood's most important job is to carry oxygen from the lungs to the muscles so they can work.

Blood is made up of a watery liquid called plasma. Most of it is made up of red blood cells. There are also white blood cells that fight disease and platelets that help blood to clot (see page 64).

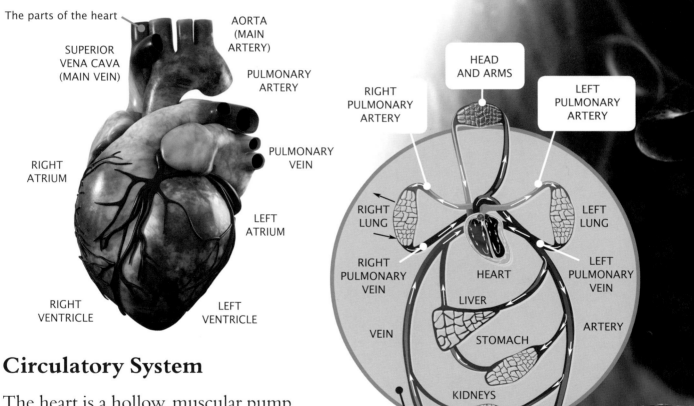

The parts of the heart

AORTA (MAIN ARTERY)

SUPERIOR VENA CAVA (MAIN VEIN)

PULMONARY ARTERY

RIGHT ATRIUM

PULMONARY VEIN

LEFT ATRIUM

RIGHT VENTRICLE

LEFT VENTRICLE

HEAD AND ARMS

RIGHT PULMONARY ARTERY

LEFT PULMONARY ARTERY

RIGHT LUNG

LEFT LUNG

RIGHT PULMONARY VEIN

HEART

LEFT PULMONARY VEIN

LIVER

VEIN

ARTERY

STOMACH

KIDNEYS

TRUNK AND LEGS

The heart pumps blood to the lungs along the pulmonary arteries. Pulmonary veins carry the oxygen-rich blood (red) back to the heart. Arteries take blood to every part of the body and veins carry oxygen-poor blood (blue) back to the heart.

Circulatory System

The heart is a hollow, muscular pump. It has two halves, left and right. Each half has an upper chamber, the atrium, and a lower chamber, the ventricle. During each heartbeat, the left atrium receives oxygen-rich blood and the left ventricle pumps it to the body. At the same time, the right atrium receives oxygen-poor blood, and the right ventricle pumps it to the lungs.

DID YOU KNOW? By some measures, the lungs are the body's largest organ—if their surface was spread out flat, it would cover about the same area as a tennis court.

Lung Structure

The lungs are two large sacs filled with branching passages that end in little pouches called alveoli. Tiny capillaries (blood vessels) wrap around the alveoli. Oxygen from air breathed into the lungs can cross the capillary membrane into the bloodstream. Carbon dioxide, a waste gas produced by muscles, can move the other way.

Red blood cells carry oxygen from the lungs and carbon dioxide to the lungs.

A muscle called the diaphragm helps us to breathe. When it contracts (pulls down), the lungs expand in size and draw in air. When it relaxes (moves up), the lungs are squeezed and air is forced out.

RELAXED DIAPHRAGM

AMAZING DISCOVERY

Scientist: William Harvey
Discovery: Circulation of blood
Date: 1628
The story: Harvey discovered veins have valves that let blood flow only one way. He realized that the heart pumps blood around the body, and that blood passes from arteries to veins through capillaries that he predicted, but could not see.

Making Babies

It takes nine months for a fertilized egg to grow into a baby that is able to survive outside its mother's body. During this time, a special organ in the woman's tummy, called the uterus or womb, provides the developing fetus with all that it needs to grow and develop.

Within the uterus, the fetus is protected inside a fluid–filled bag called the amniotic sac.

From Fertilization to Fetus

Each month between a woman's teens and early fifties, one of her ovaries releases a tiny egg. Made up of just one cell, it carries half the genetic information needed to produce another human. If it is fertilized with sperm from a man, it receives the other half of genetic material. Then it can begin to divide and become a more complex embryo. At eight weeks, it becomes a fetus.

This diagram shows an egg's journey from ovary to uterus. A sperm fertilizes the egg as it moves down the oviduct and its cells start dividing over and over. Fertilization makes the uterus lining thicken to receive the embryo. Safe in the uterus, it can develop into a baby.

1 EGG
2 FERTILIZATION
3 CELL DIVIDES
4 EMBRYO IMPLANTS
   INTO UTERUS LINING

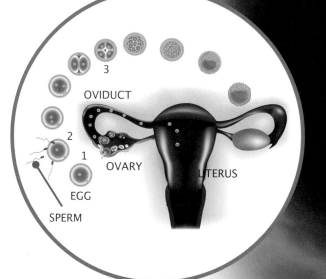

3
OVIDUCT
2
1   OVARY
EGG   UTERUS
SPERM

AMAZING DISCOVERY

Scientists: Patrick Steptoe, Robert Edwards
Discovery: IVF
Date: 1977
The story: To help a couple who couldn't conceive, these doctors put the father's sperm into the egg in a laboratory (*in vitro* fertilization, or IVF) and implanted the embryo in the mother's uterus. This was the first "test tube" baby.

The umbilical cord brings oxygen and food to the baby and takes away waste. It is connected at one end to what will become the baby's tummy button, and at the other to a spongy disk called the placenta.

An average baby weighs 2.7–4.1 kg (6–9 lb) at birth and is around 52 cm (20.5 in) long.

A Baby is Born

In the ninth month of pregnancy, the baby usually turns so that its head presses the cervix (uterus opening). The pressure encourages the uterus to begin a series of contractions (squeezes) that increase over time. Eventually, the cervix opens and the baby is pushed along the birth canal into the outside world.

Human babies are the most helpless in the animal kingdom, and need constant care. For several months, they must rely entirely on their mother's milk, before eventually moving on to solid foods.

DID YOU KNOW? In the last ten weeks of pregnancy, women need to eat about 10 percent more food.

61

Fighting Disease

Our body is under constant attack from tiny organisms called pathogens that cause disease, and it has different ways to defend itself. Waterproof skin, protective hairs, and sticky mucus form the first barrier against intruders. If any pathogens do make it through, the immune system is ready to attack.

Soldier Cells

Our immune system is made up of different types of white blood cell that can fight off invaders—neutrophils, eosinophils, basophils, lymphocytes, monocytes, and mast cells. They can engulf and digest harmful bacteria, viruses, and other microbes, or attack them with chemical weapons. Lymphocytes and monocytes work together using messengers called antibodies.

Our body can "remember" pathogens it's encountered before. Lymphocytes target them with tailor-made antibodies.

The two main types of pathogen are simple single-celled organisms called bacteria and viruses—capsules of rogue genetic information that can invade and reprogram our own cells.

VIRUS

BACTERIUM

AMAZING DISCOVERY

Scientists: Dmitri Ivanovsky, Martinus Beijerinck
Discovery: Viruses
Date: 1892–1898
The story: When Russian botanist Ivanovsky investigated a disease damaging tobacco crops, he discovered that the infection must be caused by something far smaller than a bacterium. A few years later, Beijerinck named these tiny infectious agents viruses.

DID YOU KNOW? Scientists have studied about 5,000 viruses, but there are probably millions. More than 200 of them can cause the common cold.

This organism is a flu virus. To reproduce, it needs to enter and destroy a host cell.

The lymphocyte is releasing blood proteins called antibodies that target the invaders.

These antibodies are a perfect "fit" for the flu virus. They will stick to the virus and destroy it.

Allergies

Allergic reactions happen when our immune system overreacts. Basophil, monocyte, and mast cells can all release a chemical called histamine, which makes nerve endings sensitive and itchy, increases mucus production, and swells the skin. Histamine reactions can range from a runny nose or irritating rash to a dangerously swollen airway.

A biting insect introduces microbes into the body and this can trigger the release of histamine. It's our body's way of fighting infection.

Body Repairs

Our body has an amazing ability to heal itself after it's been damaged. Wounds and broken bones repair themselves in anything from days to weeks. We can even grow new tissue for our organs, thanks to the astonishing properties of stem cells.

Clots and Scabs

When an injury breaks the skin, we bleed—and that blood helps us to heal. Tiny cells called platelets stick to the damaged tissue and cling together, slowing the flow of blood. At the same time, the wound releases chemicals that make blood thicken around the platelets and eventually form a scab.

This white line on the X-ray shows where the fracture was. Now it has healed.

This X-ray image of a ten-year-old child's wrist and lower arm bones was taken three weeks after the bone was broken.

Platelets are normally flat and plate-shaped but they change shape when they are making blood clot. They turn into "spiky" balls that bind to each other.

WHITE BLOOD CELL

RED BLOOD CELL

Fractured bone will try to heal in whatever position it ends up. The doctors made sure the ends of the bone were lined up, then placed the child's arm in a rigid cast and supportive sling while it healed.

AMAZING DISCOVERY

Scientists: James Till, Ernest McCulloch
Discovery: Stem cells
Date: 1963
The story: In their experiments on mouse bone marrow, Till and McCulloch came up with some of the first evidence of stem cells—cells that can form many types of tissue. Today we use stem cells in regenerative medicine.

Super Stem Cells

Stem cells are amazing. Doctors can introduce them to damaged organs, such as the liver, and they will start to produce replacement tissue. Scientists are also using stem cells in the laboratory to "grow" particular types of tissue, such as skin to treat patients' burns or wounds and eye tissue for people going blind.

This cornea has been grown from stem cells. It will be transplanted into a patient's eye and restore their sight.

HOW BONES HEAL

1. When a bone is fractured, blood seeps out to form a large clot.

2. A thick patch of cartilage called a callus forms over the clot.

3. The cartilage is replaced with spongy new bone to create a bony callus.

4. The bony callus hardens to form a permanent patch. It's a perfect fit.

DID YOU KNOW? The tongue and mouth lining are the fastest-healing parts of the body—they can heal from minor damage in just hours.

Physics is Everywhere

Physics tells us that the velocity or speed of the rocket will depend on its mass.

Physics is the science that explains the workings of everything in the Universe, from the tiniest to the largest scales. Its rules guide all the other branches of science, and we can see them at work everywhere in the world around us.

Understanding of physics lets us build amazing machines. We can achieve tasks as complex as launching rockets into space.

Forces and Work

We're all influenced by forces. Gravity pulls things toward the ground, while friction slows objects down when they rub together. Without forces, nothing in the Universe would ever change. A force can alter an object's speed, change its direction, or even change its shape. When a force applied to an object moves the object, that is called work. Work changes energy from one form to another or transfers energy from one object to another.

The man uses a pulling force to move the basket forward. The chemical energy in his body changes into kinetic, or movement, energy.

Other forces work on the basket, too: friction (resistance from the ground) and gravity (see pages 70–71).

AMAZING DISCOVERY

Scientist: Galileo Galilei
Discovery: Principle of relativity
Date: 1632
The story: Italian scientist Galileo's principle of relativity says it's not possible to tell whether you're on a body moving at a constant speed or a body that's not moving at all. He was thinking about whether the Earth revolves around the Sun or the Sun around the Earth.

The speed needed to escape Earth's gravity is called escape velocity. It is about 40,270 kph (25,020 mph).

The rocket keeps speeding up as long as the force pushing it up (thrust) is greater than the forces pulling it down (gravity and drag).

Made to Measure

Forces are measured in units called newtons. When we hold a 1-kg (2.2-lb) bag of sugar, we feel a downward force of almost 10 newtons thanks to the pull of gravity. Work is measured in joules. When a force of 1 newton moves an object through 1 m (3.3 ft), the work done is 1 joule.

To work out the overall forward force on this speedboat, take away the drag or friction force created by pushing through the water from the thrust force made by the engine.

DID YOU KNOW? At take-off, the space shuttle's main engines produced 1.86 million newtons of force to lift the spacecraft against the pull of Earth's gravity.

Newton's Laws of Motion

When the downward force of gravity acts on the rollercoaster, it changes its momentum.

Scientist Isaac Newton laid the foundations of modern physics with three laws of motion that he identified in the late 1600s. These laws describe the way that objects move, how they react to each other, and how forces can affect their motion.

First and Second Laws

Newton's first law says that objects will always stay still or keep moving with the same velocity (speed in one direction) unless they are affected by a force. His second law states that the bigger that force on the object, the greater the change in its momentum. Momentum is an object's mass times its velocity.

This cheetah weighs about 74 kg (163 lb), but the bull weighs ten times as much. The cheetah has a top speed or velocity five times faster than the bull, but it still has only half of its momentum.

AMANG DISCOVERY

Scientist: Isaac Newton
Discovery: Laws of motion
Date: 1679–1687
The story: Philosopher Newton wanted to understand the elongated orbits of comets around the Sun. He realized they were obeying simple laws of motion—they were being influenced by the powerful force of the Sun's gravity.

According to Newton's first law, an object stays as it is unless a force acts on it. The force that gets the rollercoaster started is provided by the mechanical chain that pulls it to its first high point.

The downward stretches of the rollercoaster ride demonstrate Newton's second law. The mass of the cars and riders combines with the force of gravity to make the cars speed up down the track.

As the riders push down on their seats, the seats push back at them in an equal and opposite reaction.

Action and Reaction

Newton's third law of motion is that an object reacts to the force acting on it. The force of this reaction is equal to the original force, but in the opposite direction. If the masses of the two objects are the same, they push away from each other at the same velocity.

When a heavy bat applies force to a lightweight ball, it boosts the ball to high velocity. The bat recoils with a much lower velocity. The velocities aren't equal because the bat and ball have different masses.

DID YOU KNOW? Newton's second law explains why objects of different masses fall at the same rate—Earth's gravity makes them speed up at a rate of 9.8 m (32.2 ft) per second, every second.

Gravity

Gravity pulls skydivers down. When their parachutes open, the force of friction will slow them down.

Gravity is the force that keeps our planet going around the Sun and keeps our feet on the ground. It is a force of attraction between objects with mass. Between small masses, it's too weak to notice. Between larger objects, gravity is so powerful that it can stretch across space and affect the shape the Universe.

The Everyday Force

Isaac Newton was the first person to suggest that the same force which makes an apple fall from a tree also keeps the Moon in orbit around the Earth. He noticed that objects with a larger mass had more gravitational pull. If two objects both have large mass, then the force between them is even stronger. However, the strength of an object's gravity gradually gets weaker as you move farther away.

EARTH

The Moon has a lower mass and smaller size than Earth. Its gravity is just one–sixth of Earth's, so astronauts can jump around there, despite their bulky spacesuits.

MOON

Gravity is pulling the aircraft toward the Earth, but its wings create a lifting force to stop it falling.

AMAZING DISCOVERY

Scientists: Robert Hooke, Isaac Newton (left)
Discovery: Universal gravitation
Date: 1666–1687
The story: Newton's rival Hooke was the first to suggest that all massive objects produce a gravitational field that stretches away into space. Newton showed that this could explain the curving orbits of planets.

Earth acts as if all its mass is at its core because it is a sphere. Its gravity pulls the skydivers toward its core.

Weightlessness

Astronauts in orbit experience weightlessness. It's not because there is no gravity on a space station. They experience almost the same pull of gravity toward Earth as we do. The difference is that everything else around them is moving at the same rate—the space station's orbital velocity, or the speed it is moving around the Earth.

Mass and weight are not the same. The skydiver's mass is how much matter their body contains. Their weight is a measure of the force of gravity acting on that mass.

This astronaut and the contents of the space station are not floating—they are falling. The station's orbital speed means it falls *around* the Earth instead of *down* to it.

Newton's second law (pages 68–69) tells us that two skydivers together fall at the same rate as one skydiver.

DID YOU KNOW? Objects called black holes have such strong gravity that nothing can ever move fast enough to escape them—not even light!

71

Waves

A wave is a disturbance that transfers energy or movement in a particular direction. Waves are everywhere in physics. The most familiar types in everyday life are water and sound waves.

Ripples spread out from the spot where the stone hit the water. These are waves and they are carrying energy. Ocean waves carry energy too.

Measuring Waves

There are three ways to measure a wave: wavelength, frequency, and amplitude. Wavelength is the distance from one peak of the wave disturbance to the next. Frequency is the number of peaks passing a single point each second. A wave's overall speed is equal to its wavelength times its frequency. Amplitude is the strength of the wave disturbance itself.

PEAK

AMPLITUDE

WAVELENGTH

TROUGH

When two waves meet, their effects add up. The waves get stronger where they line up neatly, but disappear where they don't—an effect called interference.

The ripples are evenly spaced. Each one is a separate, circular wavefront.

AMAZING DISCOVERY

Scientist: Christiaan Huygens
Discovery: Huygens' principle
Date: 1678
The story: Dutch mathematician Huygens was the first person to describe how light moves in the form of waves. He also suggested that at every point on the front of the light wave tiny wavelets spread out in all directions.

These water waves are transverse. They're carrying energy across the surface as they move up and down.

Wave Properties

There are two main types of wave: transverse and longitudinal. Each has a wavelength, frequency, and amplitude, but each moves in a different way. Nearly all waves need a material to carry them, a substance called a medium.

WAVE MOVES UP AND DOWN

DIRECTION OF TRAVEL

TRANSVERSE WAVES (eg light)
Transverse waves move in S-shaped waves. They vibrate up and down at right angles to the direction of travel.

WAVE MOVES BACK AND FORTH

DIRECTION OF TRAVEL

MEDIUM COMPRESSED

MEDIUM SPREAD OUT

LONGITUDINAL WAVES (eg sound)
Longitudinal waves move in straight lines. They vibrate back and forward along the direction of travel.

DID YOU KNOW? Sound, a longitudinal wave, travels 343 m (1,125 ft) per second at a temperature of 20°C (68°F). Light waves, which are transverse, travel almost a million times faster.

Heat and Energy

Energy is the ability to do work and make things happen. Energy cannot be created or destroyed, but is always changing from one form to another. Heat is a form of energy that makes the individual atoms in a material vibrate or jostle around. Other types of energy often get "lost" as heat, and then can't be recovered.

Forms of Energy

Energy can take many forms. Moving objects have kinetic energy. Potential energy is energy that is stored and ready to be used to do work in the future. Chemical energy is released when bonds form in a chemical reaction (see page 13).

This is a Newton's cradle. The three balls on the right have no potential energy and no kinetic energy. The ball on the left has potential energy, because it has been lifted, but no kinetic energy. When the boy releases the ball, it will move and have kinetic energy.

Heat Transfer

There are three main ways that heat energy moves from one place to another. Conduction happens in solids (see page 9). The energy travels from one atom to the next. Metals conduct heat better than wood. Convection happens in liquids and gases. It is a circular movement where hot areas expand and flow into cooler ones. Heat also travels as infrared (see page 80).

The Sun moves heat in all three ways. Conduction takes the energy from atom to atom. Convection makes hotter particles expand and rise to take the place of ones with less energy. Radiation carries the heat away into space.

AMAZING DISCOVERY

Scientists: Sadi Carnot and others
Discovery: Entropy
Date: 1824–1897
The story: In the 1800s engineers and physicists discovered that it's impossible to move energy from one form to another without losing some, often as heat. The lost energy can no longer do useful work, a state called entropy.

A single flash of lightning releases around five billion joules of energy.

Lightning heats the surrounding air to temperatures of more than 27,000°C (48,632°F).

A lightning strike has four main types of energy: electrical energy, heat, light, and sound.

DID YOU KNOW? At −273.15°C (−459.67°F), all atoms stop moving and have no kinetic energy. This is the lowest possible temperature, called absolute zero.

Electricity and Magnetism

The flow of electric current and a magnet's ability to pick up metal objects may look like very different things, but they're both aspects of a single force—electromagnetism. They both generate force fields that attract objects or push them away.

Electromagnetism at Work

Any object with electric charge generates an electromagnetic field around it, which attracts objects with the opposite charge, and repels those with the same charge. A changing electromagnetic field, meanwhile, can cause an electric current to move through a conducting material.

COILED WIRE

IRON CORE

In this simple electromagnet, electric current flows through a coiled wire to produce the magnetic field. The iron core in the middle of the coil makes the magnetic force more powerful.

AMAZING DISCOVERY

Scientist: Michael Faraday
Discovery: Electromagnetic induction
Date: 1831
The story: Faraday discovered induction while experimenting with wire coils on opposite sides of an iron ring. Passing current through one coil briefly magnetized the iron, and the changing magnetic field caused a brief current to flow in the other coil.

DID YOU KNOW? Every few hundred thousand years, the direction of Earth's magnetic field reverses completely.

This huge electromagnet's job is to move sponge iron, a form of iron ore that is used in the steel industry.

The electromagnet's magnetic field is stronger than gravity so it can lift the sponge iron.

When the electromagnet is above the place where the sponge iron is needed, its current will be turned off. It will no longer be magnetic, so the sponge iron will drop to the floor.

Magnets

The power of magnets to attract and repel metal objects has been known for around 3,000 years. A magnet is surrounded by an invisible area that has special properties. This is its magnetic field. The strength and direction of the magnetic effect is different at different spots in the field. The magnetic pull is strongest nearest to the magnet.

The metals iron and steel are magnetic materials.

Iron filings scattered around a magnet line up with the magnetic field around it. All magnets have two poles. These are named north and south to match the magnetic field of Earth itself.

Secrets of Light

Light is a form of energy that travels as a series of tiny waves. Most of our light comes from the Sun or from electric lights. It moves extremely fast—in fact, nothing in the Universe can travel faster than the speed of light.

Seeing Light

Light is a mix of wavelengths, which our eyes see as different hues. Red light has the longest wavelengths, and blue and violet have the shortest. A red T-shirt looks red because dye molecules in the fabric absorb light from the blue-violet end of the spectrum, and only red light is reflecting back.

At night, when light from the Sun does not reach us, we use artificial electric lighting. The first electric street lights were invented in 1875.

What we see as white light is made up of many hues. When white light passes through a prism, we can see this visible spectrum, which has blue and red at opposite ends.

AMAZING DISCOVERY

Scientist: Isaac Newton
Discovery: The spectrum of visible light
Date: 1672
The story: Newton split a beam of sunlight into a spectrum (rainbow) using a prism, and then brought that spectrum back together to form white light. He showed for the first time that the prism was not somehow "adding" the different hues to light.

DID YOU KNOW? Light travels at 299,793 km (186,000 miles) per second—that's fast enough to reach the Moon in around 1.3 seconds.

Tricks with Light

Light travels in a straight line from its source and bounces off objects (which lets us see them). Microscopes and telescopes use lenses to refract (bend) light and mirrors to reflect it. They can gather more light than our eyes alone, and also produce magnified images.

A magnifying glass bends the paths of light rays coming from the words. It creates a closer and larger virtual version of the words.

The light is behind this tree, which means the area in front of the tree will be in shadow.

Lights make our cities safer, but they also stop us from being able to see the night sky.

Neon lights are tubes containing neon, an element that is a gas. When electricity passes through the gas, it gives off light in a particular hue.

Invisible Rays

Visible light is just one type of electromagnetic radiation. It has a narrow range of wavelengths that our eyes can detect. Beyond it, there are other forms of radiation that are invisible to us. They carry energy from objects much hotter or colder than those that give off visible light.

Electromagnetic Spectrum

Radio waves have the longest wavelengths and come from the coolest, lowest-energy objects. We use them for broadcasting and for radio telescopes. Microwaves are next along the spectrum. We use them to send cellphone signals. Infrared radiation is produced by anything warm. Next comes visible light. Finally there are ultraviolet (UV) radiation, X-rays, and super-energetic, short-wavelength gamma rays.

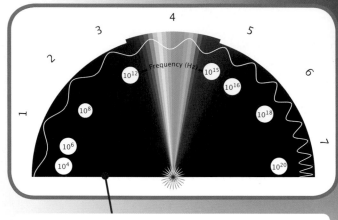

The different types of radiation are divided into a spectrum from long waves that carry little energy to short ones that carry lots. Visible light is just a small part of this electromagnetic spectrum.

RADIATION TYPES
1. RADIO WAVE
2. MICROWAVE
3. INFRARED
4. VISIBLE LIGHT
5. ULTRAVIOLET (UV)
6. X-RAY
7. GAMMA RAY

Rays in Action

The view from Earth telescopes is distorted by our atmosphere, which is why stars twinkle. Space telescopes can give astronomers a clearer view. As well as visible rays, they collect invisible rays, such as infrared, X-rays, and gamma rays from stars and other objects.

Infrared telescopes use protective shields to block the Sun, and cold gas to cool their instruments. This lets them see weak rays coming from cool dust and gas in space.

DID YOU KNOW? Radio waves have the lowest frequency in the electromagnetic spectrum and the longest wavelengths—more than 100 km (62 miles).

Scientist: William Herschel
Discovery: Infrared radiation
Date: 1800
The story: Astronomer Herschel passed light through a prism and took the temperature of each hue. Just past the red part of the spectrum, where there was no visible light, he found the temperature was even higher. He realized there must be a type of light there that we can't see. He called it infrared.

Radiation from the Sun covers the whole electromagnetic spectrum, from radio waves to gamma rays.

The body produces heat that radiates out as infrared. Protective clothing stops this heat from escaping into the atmosphere and being lost.

Goggles shield this mountaineer's eyes from harmful UV radiation from the Sun.

Hidden Forces

Four fundamental forces are responsible for every type of interaction and relationship involving matter in the Universe. Two of these, gravity and electromagnetism, work across large distances. The other two are much stronger, but are only felt on the tiny scale of particles inside the atomic nucleus.

Protons collide in special detector chambers. They are moving at 99.9 percent the speed of light.

The Large Hadron Collider (LHC) in Switzerland is the world's most powerful particle accelerator. It smashes particles together at high speed to find the building blocks of all matter, and the forces that control them.

Two beams of billions of protons shoot through the collider in opposite directions.

AMAZING DISCOVERY

Scientists: Shin'ichirō Tomonaga, Julian Schwinger, Richard Feynman
Discovery: Quantum electrodynamics
Date: 1947–1950
The story: These physicists explained the action of electromagnetism as a rapid exchange of "messenger" particles called gauge bosons, which carried force between normal matter particles. Since then, others have used the same idea to describe the two nuclear forces.

Nuclear Forces

The two forces inside the nucleus are called strong and weak (though the weak force is only weak compared to the strong one!). The strong force bonds particles called quarks to make protons and neutrons, and also holds those protons and neutrons together. The weak force can transform one kind of quark into another.

In a particle collision, the strong nuclear force works to bond them together. Its effect is stronger than the electromagnetic force that repels positively charged protons from each other.

The beams travel around a 27-km (16.8-mile) circular tunnel.

B23R2

Four Forces or One?

The four forces seem very different, but physicists believe that at least three (electromagnetism and the nuclear forces) work the same way. These forces also behave similarly in high-energy subatomic collisions such as those created at the LHC. Physicists suspect that all four forces were once united in a single "superforce."

STRONG NUCLEAR FORCE

WEAK NUCLEAR FORCE

GRAVITY

TIME AFTER BIG BANG

The superforce existed very briefly in the early Universe, where there was even more energy than in the LHC. Then the forces split from each other, but they kept certain similarities.

DID YOU KNOW? Each proton circles the LHC track more than 11,000 times a second—the equivalent of a trip to Neptune and back—before it collides with ones coming the other way.

Einstein's Universe

Newton's laws of gravity and motion describe most of physics in the everyday world, but they break down in some extreme situations. In the early 1900s, Albert Einstein came up with an idea called relativity that offered a more accurate picture of how the Universe really works.

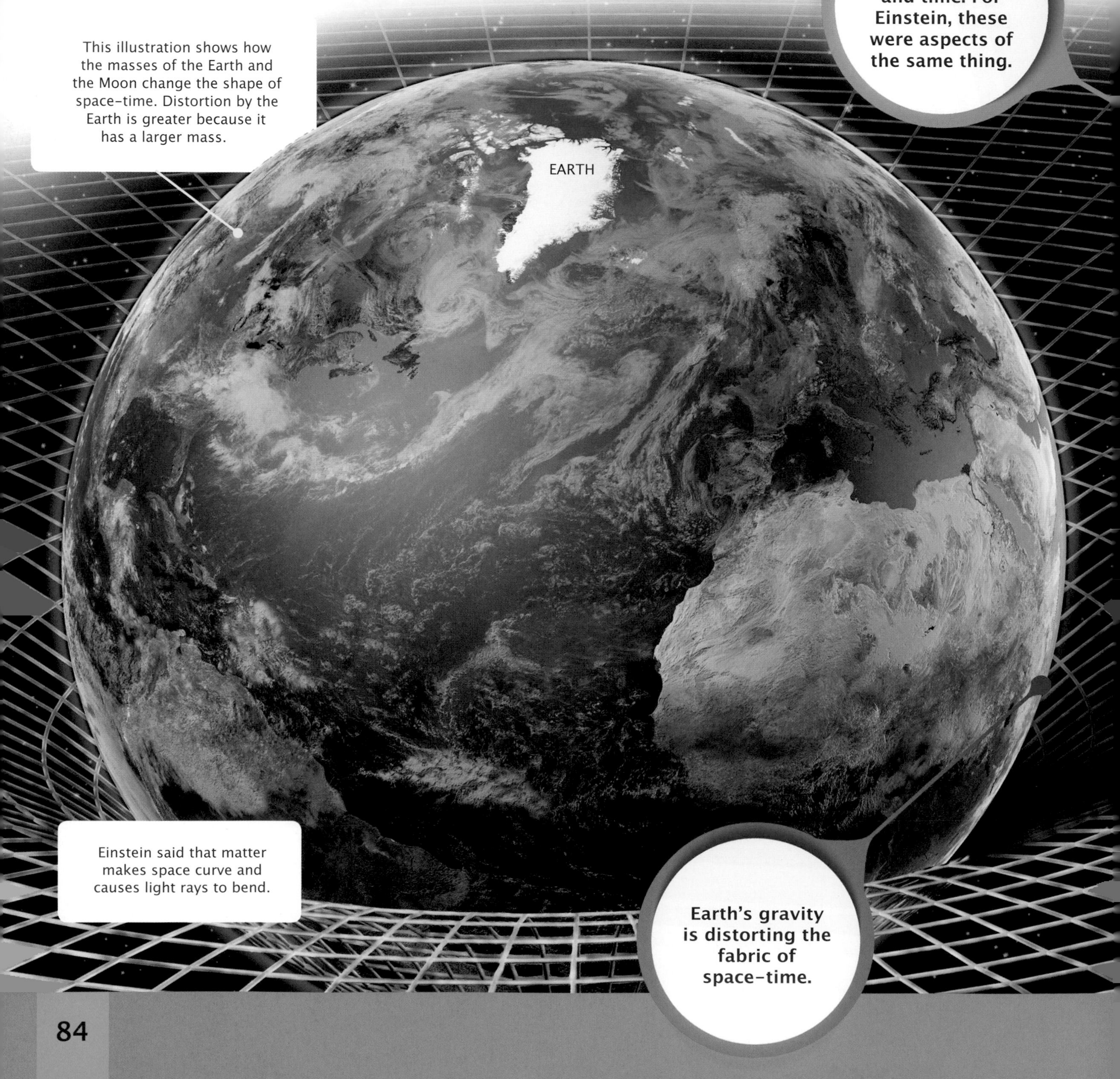

This illustration shows how the masses of the Earth and the Moon change the shape of space–time. Distortion by the Earth is greater because it has a larger mass.

This matrix represents space and time. For Einstein, these were aspects of the same thing.

EARTH

Einstein said that matter makes space curve and causes light rays to bend.

Earth's gravity is distorting the fabric of space–time.

Special and General Relativity

Einstein's special theory of relativity (1905) describes how physics changes when objects travel at speeds close to the speed of light. His general theory (1915) sets out how physics behaves in situations with extreme gravity. Einstein explained that space has a structure that can be warped out of shape by large masses.

German-born Einstein was just 26 years old when he published his special theory of relativity.

MOON

Distortions of space-time caused by large masses such as Earth hold smaller ones like the Moon in orbit around them

Blue light from a distant galaxy has its path changed as it passes nearer galaxies (yellow) that are bending space around them. The light reaches Earth as a series of distorted images.

Proofs of Relativity

The ideas of special and general relativity have been proved in many experiments. Special relativity causes clocks carried on fast-moving satellites to run more slowly than those that remain on Earth. General relativity explains how large masses can deflect the path of light that passes close to them.

AMAZING DISCOVERY

Scientist: Arthur Eddington
Discovery: Gravitational lensing
Date: 1919
The story: By photographing a total solar eclipse (when the Moon briefly hides the disc of the Sun), Eddington showed how the Sun's gravity deflects the path of starlight, proving Einstein's theory of general relativity.

DID YOU KNOW? Astronauts on a six-month mission to the International Space Station age about 0.007 seconds less than if they stayed on Earth because of their orbital speed.

Simple Machines

Ramps, wedges, levers, wheels and axles, screws, and pulleys are all simple machines that people have used since ancient times. Ramps and wedges might not seem like machines, but they are. Machines are devices that use the laws of physics to make tasks easier.

Making Work Easier

Doing any physical task involves work—in other words, applying a force to an object that moves it. The amount of work for a particular job is always the same, but a machine makes it easier. The machine multiplies the amount of force we apply, or it increases the distance over which the force acts.

Even before the invention of the axle, the people who built Stonehenge may have used basic wheels—sledges on rolling logs—to move massive stones.

Simple to Modern

Ancient inventors found many ingenious ways to power their simple machines. They used the weight of falling water, the movement of tides, and the force of wind. Modern machines date from the Industrial Revolution. In 1712, Thomas Newcomen built the first successful steam engine, which used the force of expanding or condensing steam to power machines.

This 1834 engraving shows a textile factory with steam–powered printing machines. Steam was used in industry till the early 1900s, when electricity began to take over.

The farther away the swings are from the axle, the faster they move.

The swings are attached to a wheel. The wheel turns when force is applied to the central axle.

A wheel won't work without an axle—a central rod or cylinder that it can turn around. The wheel and axle work together to help things move. The force can be applied to the wheel or the axle.

A motor moves the axle. The circle turned by the wheel is much larger than the circle turned by the axle.

AMAZING DISCOVERY

Scientist: Archimedes
Discovery: Machines of war
Date: 213 BCE
The story: Greek mathematician Archimedes built pulley systems, cranes, catapults, and other machines to help defend his home city against invading Roman ships in 213 BCE. He also wrote the first proper explanations of the science behind such machines.

DID YOU KNOW? An ax's wedge-shaped head is a simple machine. Force applied to the thick end becomes concentrated in the thin edge so that it has enough pressure to chop.

Engines, Motors, and Generators

Engines are machines that use one form of energy (such as heat or electricity) to produce another—motion energy that can do work. Steam, petrol, and diesel engines all burn fuels to create this energy. Electric motors rely on electricity and magnetism.

Electric Motors

An electric motor works because of the relationship between permanent magnets and an electromagnet. A spinning rotor sits in a drum lined with fixed magnets called stators. Alternating current passes through coiled wires around the rotor. It produces a changing magnetic field that pushes the coil away from the stators.

High-performance vehicles like this rally car use winglike stabilizers called spoilers. These create downforce and push them into the ground.

The car's body is built around a roll cage—a superstrong framework that protects the driver if the car crashes.

To keep spinning in the same direction, the electric current in the motor's coils must be constantly changing.

AMAZING DISCOVERY

Scientist: Ányos Jedlik
Discovery: Spinning electric motor
Date: 1828
The story: Hungarian scientist Jedlik came up with the key to a working electric motor. He worked out that changing the direction of current flowing inside an an electric coil would keep it spinning in a ring of magnets.

Generating Turbines

Turbines are one of the most common ways of producing electricity. They work like an electric motor in reverse. Motion energy spins a wire-wrapped rotor in a magnetic field and makes current flow in the rotor wires. The motion energy can come from expanding steam, water falling from a dam, ocean waves, or gusts of wind.

This cutaway shows the insides of a wind turbine, which makes "green" or renewable electricity. The motion energy comes from the wind turning the blades.

A combustion engine turns chemical energy (the combustion, or burning, of fuel) into mechanical power.

Most car engines burn gasoline/petrol (ignited by an electric spark) or diesel fuel (ignited by compressed hot air).

DID YOU KNOW? The world's tiniest electric motor is just one–36,000th of the width of a human hair. It was built from a single molecule in 2011.

89

Electronics

Electronics are built into our televisions, smartphones, games consoles, laptops, and e-books. Everyday appliances such as washing machines and dishwashers rely on them too. Electronic devices control and adjust the flow of small numbers of electrons in an electric current. They can use the electric current to represent some kind of signal or information.

Electronic Components

The first electronic devices were amplifiers that could boost weak currents to useful levels. These amplifiers were like valves, and made current flow in only one direction. The same technology made radios and computers possible. Today's valves, called diodes and triodes, are incredibly small. They are made using materials called semiconductors.

A CD player's lens directs intense laser light created by a special diode onto the reflecting surface of a CD.

Tiny pits cover the disc. These dots or dashes represent digital information such as games, music, or pictures.

Adding other elements to these thin wafers of silicon will turn them into semiconductors. A semiconductor creates a barrier that lets current flow in only one direction.

AMAZING DISCOVERY

Scientists: John Ambrose Fleming, William Shockley
Discovery: Valves and transistors
Date: 1904, 1947
The story: In 1904 Fleming invented a lightbulb–like device called the valve diode, which caused a strong current to flow one way when a weak current was received. In 1947 Shockley used semiconductor materials to build tiny transistors that did the same thing.

DID YOU KNOW? A string of eight bits can represent any number from 0 to 255. 64 bits can represent any number up to 9,223,372,036,854,775,807.

Analog and Digital

Analog electronics uses currents that change strength to transmit their signal, but electrical interference can damage the signal. Digital electronics isn't affected by electrical interference. It uses currents with just two possible values (the numbers 1 or 0—also known as "bits"). The system where 1s and 0s can stand for any number is called binary.

The pits reflect the beam in different directions. A light-detector converts the flickering beam into electric current.

The digital electronic display on a car dashboard shows the driver information, such as speed of travel or even navigational maps.

Computers

At its most basic, a computer is a device that does simple calculations very quickly, even for very large numbers, and identifies patterns in the numbers. By adding clever design and programing to this basic mathematical ability, we now have computers that can carry out a mind-boggling variety of different tasks.

The Brain

The computer's central processing unit (CPU) "reads" information stored in the computer's memory, performs calculations, and then "writes" results back to other parts of the memory. Electronic components called logic gates let the CPU do mathematics and make decisions based on binary numbers (strings of 1s and 0s).

Although computers are great for games, they can also make difficult and repetitive tasks much easier.

Built between 1943 and 1946, room–sized ENIAC was one of the first digital computers. It could carry out 5,000 instructions a second.

AMAZING DISCOVERY

Scientists: Charles Babbage, Ada Lovelace
Discovery: The analytical engine
Date: 1837, 1843
The story: In 1837, long before electronics, English inventor Babbage designed a universal computing machine using brass wheels. It was never built, but mathematician Lovelace worked out the commands needed to run it, making her the first computer programmer. She published her findings in 1843.

DID YOU KNOW? An iPhone X processes 600 billion instructions per second.

Computer Memory

Computers store information they need fast access to on memory chips. Basic operating instructions are written on permanent Read-Only Memory (ROM) chips. Less urgent data, such as applications or the user's files, is saved on a slower magnetic hard disc and then moved to faster Random Access Memory (RAM) chips when it's needed.

A computer's motherboard connects up all of its various components, including the CPU, ROM and RAM memory chips, and hard disc drive.

Special computer circuits can create sounds from digital files.

Special graphics processors (GPUs) create realistic moving images on the screen.

A mouse lets the computer user highlight and manipulate items on the screen.

Connected World

Hylas 1, a communications satellite, circles the Earth in the same time it takes Earth to spin on its axis. Its orbit is 35,800 km (22,245 miles) above the equator.

Our phones, televisions, Internet, and many other modern technologies rely on computers and other machines being able to talk to each other over huge distances. They communicate by sending their signals through networks of wires or cables or by beaming them through the air in electromagnetic radio waves.

Sending Signals

We send analog signals in two forms. We can use electric current, changing or modulating its strength to transmit the signal; or we can use radio waves, and change their shape. Either way, a receiver decodes the patterns to work out the signal. Today, however, most signals are sent digitally. The information is converted into streams of binary numbers, and sent between machines as 1s and 0s.

HYLAS 1

Satellites such as *Hylas 1* are solar-powered—they generate their electricity from sunlight.

A phone mast can beam out hundreds of calls at the same time. The signals are digital so they cannot get mixed up like the "crossed wires" of the past.

94

Pulses of Light

In the past, we sent information along fixed cables as electrical signals. Today we use laser beams to send information along glass optical fibers as pulses of light instead. The pulses keep their strength over long distances, but most networks also include repeaters—devices that boost the signal.

Dish-shaped antennae send and receive signals to and from Earth.

Communications satellites receive radio signals from one part of the Earth and beam them to another.

Optical fibers are thin, bendy strands of glass. They carry information in the form of pulses of laser light.

AMAZING DISCOVERY

Scientists: Hedy Lamarr, George Anthiel
Discovery: Spread-spectrum
Date: 1941
The story: Hollywood actor Lamarr and composer Anthiel invented a secure system for encoding data in radio signals called the spread-spectrum technique. It is the basis of modern wireless systems such as Bluetooth.

DID YOU KNOW? Signals have been successfully sent more than 10,000 km (6,214 miles) along optical fibers without using repeaters to boost them.

Flying Machines

Humans have always dreamed of taking to the air. In the 1780s the French Montgolfier brothers became the first to achieve this with their hot-air balloons. However, powered and steerable flight only became possible in the 20th century.

Like a Bird

Powered aircraft have birdlike wings that generate an upward force called lift. The wing's shape creates a difference in the air pressure above and below that pushes it upward. Aircraft wings can't flap like a bird's, so they must move much faster through the air to keep the plane off the ground.

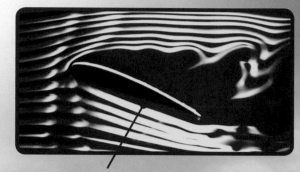

This image of a wing being tested in a wind tunnel shows how air is forced faster over the upper surface. Adjusting the shape and angle of the wing affects the amount of lift.

Up, Up, and Away

Helicopters produce lift with their rotor blades—spinning wings that cut through the air without the entire aircraft needing to move. The fast-moving tail blade generates a sideways force that stops the machine from spinning with its main rotor.

Helicopters can take off and land vertically. The pilot adjusts the angle of each spinning blade to alter the amount of lift it produces, and tilts the entire rotor to push the helicopter forward.

The fuselage (aircraft body) of metal alloys and other materials is both strong and light.

The bullet-shaped nose reduces drag, helping the aircraft cut through the air at high speed.

Jet engines use spinning blades to compress air before using it to burn fuel. Hot exhaust gases blown out of the engines push the aircraft forward.

Flaps on the wings adjust their shape to alter how much lift they create.

AMAZING DISCOVERY

Scientists: Orville and Wilbur Wright
Discovery: Aircraft controls
Date: 1903–1905
The story: The American Wright brothers invented controls that let them control the precise angle of an aircraft in the air, and the shape of its wings. This helped them to make the first powered, controlled flight in 1903.

DID YOU KNOW? Russia's Antonov An-225 is the world's biggest aircraft, with a wingspan of 88.4 m (262.5 ft). It can carry up to 250 tonnes (550,000 lb) of cargo.

Smart Materials

Some materials can react to their surroundings in a useful way. Smart materials change when they are exposed to something like temperature, light, pressure, electricity, or a magnetic field. They already have many uses, and they'll become even more common in the future.

Materials with Memory

Some of the most amazing smart materials are alloys (metal mixtures) and plastics with built-in "memory." They can be crushed or reshaped, but they change back to their original state when they are "told to"—for example, if they are heated or dampened.

NASA scientists hope to build aircraft with smart wings. The idea is that the wings could sense alterations in air pressure and change their shape to suit flying conditions.

AMAZING DISCOVERY

Scientists: William J Buehler, David S. Muzzey
Discovery: Nitinol
Date: 1962
The story: Buehler, a researcher at the US Naval Ordinance Laboratory, discovered this nickel–titanium mix. Its smart properties were discovered by chance in a laboratory meeting, when Muzzey held a lighter under a bent sample and found it slowly returned to its original shape.

DID YOU KNOW? Shape-memory alloys have to be "trained" into their original shape. Nitinol is heated to 500°C (932°F) for 30 minutes, shaped, and then rapidly cooled.

Smart Power

Photovoltaic (PV) semiconductors (solar panels) are among the smartest materials humans have ever made. They make electricity for us from sunlight. Their atoms lose electrons when they are exposed to photons (light particles)—the electrons flow to an electrode as current. PV materials react to temperature change.

We use PV semiconductors in solar panels for making pollution-free energy on Earth, and for powering satellites and spacecraft.

The metal in these spectacles can be bent and twisted, but always returns to its original shape.

If you squash superelastic metal, it changes its crystal structure. However, when the pressure is released, the new structure will become unstable and change back to its original form.

Nuclear Energy

Compared to its size, the forces at work inside an atom's central nucleus are enormous. Nuclear power plants tap into this huge energy source. They use a process called nuclear fission that makes some heavy, unstable atoms split into smaller, more stable forms.

Nuclear Fission

Fission happens all the time in nature. Nuclei of elements such as uranium are naturally unstable or "radioactive." They disintegrate at random, releasing small bursts of energy. Nuclear power harnesses this process by creating a chain reaction. Each disintegration instantly triggers several more, and a trickle of energy turns into a torrent.

The US National Ignition Facility (NIF) houses the world's largest, most energetic laser. It hopes to copy the nuclear fusion going on in the Sun to provide an unlimited, cheap source of electricity.

Nuclear power plants use the energy they release to turn water into steam. The steam drives electricity–producing turbines and then escapes through huge cooling towers.

In a fission chain reaction, a neutron particle (1) strikes an unstable atom (2), making it split apart (3). The fission process leaves behind smaller nuclei (4) and more neutrons (5), and so the nuclear reaction can start all over again.

Future Fusion?

Fusion reactions release energy by joining lightweight nuclei instead of breaking apart heavy ones. Unlike fission, fusion does not involve rare heavy elements and doesn't leave behind long-lasting pollution. It sounds like a recipe for cheap, clean energy, but the problem is that fusion only takes place at temperatures like those in the core of the Sun.

The laser beams in the NIF surround a pellet of hydrogen fuel. They compress and heat it to the point where nuclear fusion takes place.

The NIF aims to start a reaction that keeps going on its own—a goal no fusion experiment has yet achieved.

AMAZING DISCOVERY

Scientists: Lise Meitner, Otto Hahn
Discovery: Nuclear fission
Date: 1938
The story: Meitner and Hahn discovered that uranium atoms will decay when struck by smaller neutron particles, releasing energy. Because uranium decay also releases neutrons, it is the key to a nuclear chain reaction.

DID YOU KNOW? Fission uses rare forms of elements called isotopes. A small sample of the uranium 235 isotope generates 3.7 million times more energy than the same amount of coal.

Nanotechnology

Imagine machines made up of individual atoms, able to copy themselves, assemble objects, and even repair our bodies or fight disease at a molecular level. This is the idea behind nanotechnology—and while this new science hasn't yet delivered all these dreams, it is already starting to affect our everyday lives.

Teeny-Tiny Tech

Nanotechnology involves building on the scale of nanometers (billionths of 1 m/3.3 ft) or less. Nanomaterials are substances with engineered atomic-scale structures that give them useful properties. We already use them to make self-cleaning glass, dirt-repellent paints and sprays, and superfine filters for purifying water and trapping viruses.

Carbon nanotubes can be used in touch-screen devices, such as tablets, and high-strength bullet-proof vests.

Building with Atoms

Nanoengineers can also build structures out of individual atoms. They use a machine called an atomic force microscope to "see" the separate atoms on a material—and they can even pick them up and move them around! This technology could eventually let us build complex computers atom by atom.

Scanning tunneling microscopes are the best way of mapping and building with single atoms.

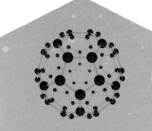

AMAZING DISCOVERY

Scientists: Richard Smalley, Robert Curl, Harold Kroto
Discovery: Fullerenes
Date: 1985
The story: Smalley, Curl, and Kroto led a team of chemists who discovered a ball of carbon atoms that they called buckminsterfullerene. This was the first hint that carbon could create strong rings and tubes for use in nanotechnology.

Nanoparticles packed with anti-cancer drugs are being tested for use in the future.

Scientists hope that nanotreatments like this will one day be a reality.

When the nanoparticles are heated by laser beam, they burst and release anti-cancer drugs.

CANCER CELL

Cancers form when healthy cells mutate and begin to reproduce out of control.

ANTI-CANCER DRUGS

NANOPARTICLE

The anti-cancer nanoparticles are injected into a blood vessel.

Nanoparticles leak out of the blood vessel, into a cancerous cell, and release their drugs.

DID YOU KNOW? The nanoengineers who built "geckotape" were inspired by the billions of nanoscale hairs on a gecko's feet. It sticks to any surface using forces between molecules.

Genetic Engineering

Crops can be given genes from other organisms which carry benefits such as resistance to pests or drought.

Genetic engineering lets scientists alter the genes of living things, from plants and animals to human beings. Selecting DNA molecules that carry specific genes can have exciting results, such as preventing diseases. But it also raises a tricky question: will we clone humans? And would the clones be truly human?

Engineering Methods

Simple genetic selection helps to avoid inherited diseases. Doctors fertilize a woman's eggs in a laboratory, check them for the disease-causing gene, then implant disease-free eggs into her uterus. A more complicated technique, known as gene editing, replaces parts of a particular DNA strand that carry faulty genes.

Gene editing involves using a pair of chemical "scissors" to enter the cell and replace the faulty DNA. The corrected DNA strand is then copied each time the cell reproduces.

Cloning

Clones are organisms that have identical genes. Geneticists replace the nucleus of an egg cell with one from a donor individual. The new nucleus divides and reproduces to create stem cells—special cells that can create or repair any kind of body tissue. The resulting clone has all the same genes as the donor.

The first and most famous cloned mammal was a sheep called Dolly. She is shown here with Ian Wilmut, who helped to create her.

Genetically modified (GM) food is allowed in some countries but not in others. Some people have doubts about eating it, but there's no evidence it causes harm.

Scientists must take care that GM crops do not breed with other farmers' normal crops.

AMAZING DISCOVERY

Scientists: Ian Wilmut, Keith Campbell, the Roslin Institute
Discovery: How to clone a mammal
Date: 1996
The story: Wilmut, Campbell, and their team created Dolly by injecting the nucleus of a cell from a Finn–Dorset sheep into an egg cell from a Scottish Blackface. Then they implanted the embryo into a Blackface surrogate mother.

DID YOU KNOW? In 2012 scientists in Utah used genetic modification to create goats whose milk includes the same proteins as super-strong spider silk.

Inside the Earth

Our planet is a huge ball of rock, 12,742 km (7,918 miles) across. It might seem solid all the way through, but not far beneath the surface is a deep layer called the mantle, which is a mix of semi-molten and solid rock. Deeper still, Earth's core is a swirling ball of molten and solid metal.

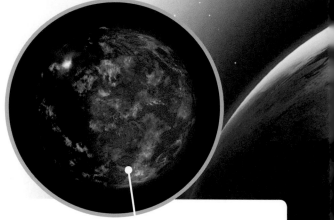

Earth was born about 4.6 billion years ago out of material left over from making the Sun. At first, even the surface was hot, molten rock. Our planet has been slowly cooling down ever since.

Layers within Layers

Earth's crust floats on the upper, semi-molten part of the mantle, and is cracked into giant plates. Rocks churn and grind past each other in the mantle, carrying heat from the core to the surface. The superhot core is made of iron and nickel, and mostly molten but solid at its heart.

Earth's Magnetic Field

The liquid part of Earth's metal core produces huge electric currents as it swirls, and these create a magnetic field. It is as if our planet is a giant magnet, with magnetic north and south poles close to the axis of its spin. This magnetic field forms a bubble around the Earth, which we call the magnetosphere.

The magnetosphere repels dangerous particles from the Sun. Harmless, lower-energy solar particles fall into the atmosphere over the magnetic poles to create aurorae (see page 109).

AMANZING DISCOVERY

Scientist: Andrija Mohorovicic
Discovery: Earth's internal layers
Date: 1909
The story: Scientist Mohorovicic observed that earthquake shockwaves change their speed depending on their depth below the surface. He realized this was because they passed through different rock types and temperatures.

The thickness of Earth's crust ranges from 3-5 km (2-3 miles) to as much as 70 km (44 miles).

The mantle is made of similar rocks to Earth's crust but with more metals, such as iron and magnesium.

The oceans lie on top of the crust in low-lying basins. Earth's gravity traps a layer of protective gases, the atmosphere, above it.

The outer core is made of liquid iron and nickel, with a solid middle of superhot metal.

The mantle is 2,900 km (1,800 miles) deep, so it makes up most of Earth's interior. Heat rising from the core makes some of its rocks churn like thick, slow-moving liquid.

DID YOU KNOW? Geologists estimate that the boundary between Earth's solid inner and liquid outer cores is 6,000°C (10,832°F)—hotter than the surface of the Sun.

Atmosphere and Weather

Earth is surrounded by a thin but vital layer of gas called the atmosphere. It provides the air we breathe, creates a protective blanket that keeps out the worst extremes of hot and cold, and give us a complex system of ever-changing weather.

Atmospheric Gases

Without an atmosphere absorbing and trapping the Sun's heat, our planet would be unbearably hot in the day and icy-cold at night. The main gases in the atmosphere are nitrogen and oxygen. Oceans, rocks, and life absorb and produce different gases, creating a delicate balance.

Weather happens in the troposphere, the layer of the atmosphere that is closest to the Earth.

1. Warm air rises near the equator, cools, and sinks down closer to poles.

2. Winds are driven by the Earth's rotation, and by rising and falling air.

AMAZING DISCOVERY

Scientist: George Hadley
Discovery: Atmospheric circulation and winds
Date: 1735
The story: Amateur meteorologist (weather scientist) Hadley was the first person to realize that wind patterns were due to the Earth spinning on its axis and the way air rises in hot areas and sinks in colder ones.

Aurorae, also known as the northern and southern lights, happen close to the poles. Earth's magnetic field attracts tiny particles from space.

Oxygen atoms glow green at low altitudes and red at high ones. Nitrogen produces blue or purple.

Most aurorae are in the thermosphere. They happen 80–640 km (50–400 miles) above the ground.

Balancing the Climate

Carbon dioxide (CO_2) is called a greenhouse gas because it traps heat like the glass of a greenhouse. The CO_2 in our atmosphere keeps our planet warm. However, burning fossil fuels such as coal and oil creates more CO_2 than there used to be. This is heating the planet at a faster rate and changing our climate.

The atmosphere is divided into layers that stretch out into space. It gets thinner the higher we go.

1. TROPOSPHERE up to 12 km (7.5 miles)
2. STRATOSPHERE 12–50 km (7.5–31 miles)
3. MESOSPHERE 50–80 km (31–50 miles)
4. THERMOSPHERE 80–700 km (50–435 miles)
5. EXOSPHERE 700–10,000 km (435–6,214 miles)

DID YOU KNOW? At the outer edge of the exosphere, 10,000 km (6,214 miles) above Earth's surface, lightweight gas particles are constantly blown away into space.

Earth's Water

Earth is the only world in our solar system with the right surface temperature for water to exist as liquid, solid ice, and gas (water vapor). The water cycle changes water between these forms, moves it around, and shapes our planet.

Water naturally flows downhill. Rainfall over land finds its way to the oceans through rivers, lakes, and underground springs.

Erosion

Water is an irresistible force. Rivers and slow-moving bodies of ice called glaciers wear away and erode Earth's rocks. Seas beat at cliffs. Over thousands of years, water shapes the landscape and transports ground-down particles, or sediment, into low-lying areas. Water is an even more powerful erosive force than wind or extreme hot or cold.

The Grand Canyon in Arizona is an 1,800 m/1.1 mile-deep valley. It has been carved out by the winding Colorado River over the past six million years or more.

AMAZING DISCOVERY

Scientist: Benjamin Franklin
Discovery: The Gulf Stream
Date: 1769–1770
The story: The Gulf Stream current of warm, fast-moving water flowing north and east across the Atlantic was known to earlier sailors, but Franklin was first to study it in detail. He saw it was part of a bigger pattern of ocean movements.

Where winter snowfall does not completely melt in summer, it builds up into creeping layers of ice called glaciers.

Up to four percent of Earth's atmosphere is water vapor. When vapor condenses to form clouds in the air, droplets can fall to the ground as rain or snow.

Water Distribution

Most water is mixed with salty minerals in Earth's seas. Fresh water makes up just 3.5 percent, and most of it is frozen into ice around the poles and on high mountains. Liquid fresh water is found in lakes, rivers, and underground. There is also a small but vital amount of water vapor in the atmosphere.

Rain falls. It flows downhill thanks to gravity.

Clouds carry moisture back over land.

Water evaporates from sea into air.

Water flows back to the sea.

Heat from the Sun drives ocean water into the air as moisture. It returns to the ground as rain and snow, creating rivers and lakes and shaping the landscape as it flows back to the sea.

Ice caps like the ones over Greenland and Antarctica trap frozen water on top of land.

DID YOU KNOW? If all of Earth's water was collected into a ball, it would be about 1,385 km (860.6 miles) across—just 0.1 percent of our planet's entire volume.

Earth's Crust

Earth's crust is part of what makes our planet unique. It is broken into seven major plates (and many smaller ones) that move around on top of the slowly churning mantle. Over millions of years these plates rearrange Earth's continents and oceans in a process that is called plate tectonics.

Where plates in the crust pull apart, thin new crust is produced by volcanic eruptions from the mantle.

Floating Continents

The crust floats on top of the mantle because it is made of lighter rocks. Where the crust is highest (on continents or at high mountain ranges), it also stretches down the deepest—rather like an iceberg. Continental crust can be up to 70 km (44 miles) thick.

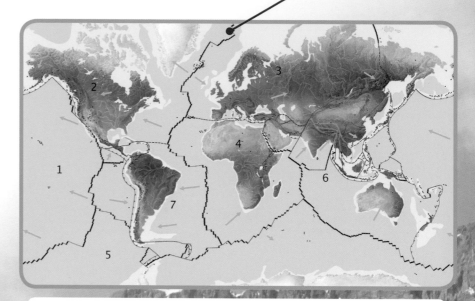

MAJOR TECTONIC PLATES
1. PACIFIC PLATE 2. NORTH AMERICAN PLATE 3. EURASIAN PLATE
4. AFRICAN PLATE 5. ANTARCTIC PLATE
6. INDO–AUSTRALIAN PLATE (broken into Australian and Indian plates)
7. SOUTH AMERICAN PLATE

Places such as China's Striped Mountains show how sedimentary rock forms in strata, or layers.

Three Types of Rock

Igneous rocks, such as basalt, form from cooled magma, either underground or where it's erupted as lava from a volcano. Sedimentary rocks, such as sandstone, are made when ground-down particles of rock settle and compress. Metamorphic rocks are created when another kind of rock is put under great heat or pressure, changing the minerals it contains—heated limestone becomes marble, for example.

Some mountains are made from igneous rocks that solidified from molten lava.

Even the highest mountains are steadily worn away over time by heat, cold, wind, and rain.

Some mountains contain rocks that formed on the seabed millions of years ago.

AMAZING DISCOVERY

Scientist: James Hutton
Discovery: Cycles in Earth's history
Date: 1785
The story: Scottish geologist Hutton showed how the three main types of rock relate to each other because of repeated cycles of settling, lifting up, and wearing away, stretching back over hundreds of millions of years.

DID YOU KNOW? Most tectonic plates move around 2.5 cm (1 in) per year, but the South Pacific Nazca plate is racing along more than twice as fast.

Volcanoes and Earthquakes

Powerful forces are unleashed in places where the plates of Earth's crust come together. Huge masses of rock crumple against or grind past each other and trigger devastating earthquakes. Where crust is driven down into the mantle, molten rock escapes through chains of volcanoes.

Violent eruptions happen when trapped gas bursts from pockets of magma beneath Earth's surface.

Plate Boundaries

If plates meet head-on, what happens next depends on the types of crust involved. Thin ocean crust will be pushed under thick continental crust, and as it melts in the mantle it will release heat that creates volcanoes. Where two continental plates meet, they buckle to create towering mountain ranges.

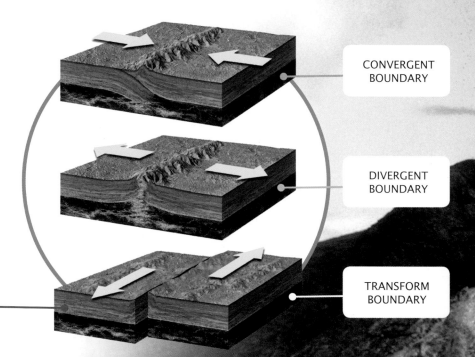

CONVERGENT BOUNDARY

DIVERGENT BOUNDARY

TRANSFORM BOUNDARY

Plates collide at convergent boundaries, pull apart (often beneath the oceans) at divergent boundaries, and grind past each other at transform boundaries.

AMAZING DISCOVERY

Scientist: Alfred Wegener
Discovery: Tectonic drift
Date: 1912
The story: Meteorologist Wegener noticed how the edges of widely separated landmasses fit together like a jigsaw. He suggested that continents move slowly around on Earth's crust, but his idea only began to be accepted in the 1950s.

Volcanoes form where tectonic movements heat and melt underground rock to form molten magma. When magma erupts at the surface, it is called lava.

Earthquakes

When Earth's crust suddenly shifts, it triggers waves of disturbance called earthquakes. This can happen when tectonic plates collide or when they grind sideways past each other. The waves spread through the crust and also down through the Earth. Sometimes the vibrations can be detected on the other side of the world.

Many of our biggest cities, such as Mexico City, are built in earthquake zones. Unfortunately scientists cannot yet predict exactly where or when a disastrous quake will strike.

Liquid lava from volcanoes cools down rapidly. It solidifies into new igneous rocks.

Volcanoes and earthquakes happen at plate boundaries, and also above random "hot spots" in Earth's mantle.

DID YOU KNOW? The 1883 eruption of the Krakatoa volcano in Indonesia was the loudest sound in recorded history. People heard the explosion 5,000 km (3,100 miles) away!

Earth and Moon

Earth is not alone on its journey through space. A rocky satellite world we call the Moon orbits our planet every 27.3 days. At 3,474 km (2,160 miles) across, the Moon is a quarter of Earth's diameter. It is up to 400,000 km (248,548 miles) away—close enough to have a great influence on our planet.

A Lifeless World

The Moon's small size and gravity mean it cannot hold onto an atmosphere, and it has no life, surface water, or tectonic plates. Its main features are bright highlands and dark, smooth "seas" of solidified lava from ancient volcanoes. The highlands are covered in craters from when the Moon was bombarded by space rocks early in its history.

Volcanic activity ended on the Moon about three billion years ago. Since then, only a few new craters have appeared from asteroid impacts.

Dust thrown out during asteroid impacts forms bright streaks across the surface.

The Moon doesn't have its own light—it reflects the Sun's. As it orbits us, we see different amounts of the lit-up side and it seems to change shape. The different shapes are called the phases of the Moon.

AMAZING DISCOVERY

Scientists: The *Apollo* astronauts
Discovery: Origins of the Moon
Date: 1969–1972
The story: Rocks collected during the *Apollo* Moon landings showed scientists back on Earth how the Moon was made. It probably formed from molten rock ejected when a Mars-sized world collided with the young Earth 4.51 billion years ago.

DID YOU KNOW? Energy from Earth's tides makes the Moon move about 3.8 cm (1.5 in) farther away from us each year.

The Moon has no air to protect it. Temperatures range from 127°C (260°F) in sunlight to −173°C (−280°F) in darkness.

Darker "seas" show where volcanic lava filled huge craters on the Moon's surface.

Time and Tide

The Moon's gravity pulls on the near side of Earth. This creates bulges in Earth's oceans directly beneath, and opposite, the Moon. As Earth rotates each day under these bulges, the seas rise and fall.

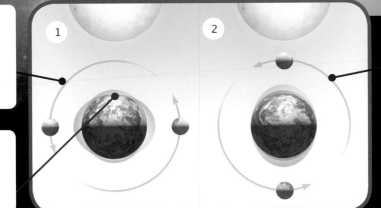

Tidal bulges cancel each other out, resulting in weak tides.

Tidal bulges join together, resulting in especially strong tides.

The Sun's gravity creates its own tidal bulge. It can either work against the Moon's pull (1) or with it (2).

Solar System

Earth is the third of eight planets orbiting our local star, the Sun. The part of space caught in the Sun's pull is called the solar system. As well as the planets, it contains countless smaller worlds—rocky asteroids in the inner solar system, and frozen comets and ice dwarfs farther out.

The Planets

Mercury, Venus, Earth, and Mars are closest to the Sun. Earth is the largest of these rocky planets. Farther out lie the giant planets— Jupiter (the biggest of all), Saturn, Uranus, and Neptune. Each of the giant planets has rings and a family of moons.

NEPTUNE

URANUS

Saturn's bright ring system is made up of countless icy fragments in orbit around it.

The Sun is a massive, fiery ball of gas, about 1.4 million km (870,000 miles) across. It contains 99.8 percent of the solar system's mass, and it provides heat and light to all of the planets.

AMAZING DISCOVERY

Scientists: Tycho Brahe, Johannes Kepler
Discovery: Orbits of the planets
Date: 1572–1619
The story: Kepler used Brahe's careful observations of Mars to show that planets do not move in perfect circles. He explained that their paths are elliptical (stretched), and that they move faster when they are closer to the Sun.

Edge of the Solar System

Neptune's orbit takes it 30 times farther from the Sun than Earth, but this is not the edge of the solar system. Beyond this outermost planet lies the Kuiper Belt, a ring of small, icy worlds including Pluto. And beyond that is the Oort Cloud, a shell of icy comets that is 100,000 times Earth's distance from the Sun.

Icy comets are sometimes pushed into orbits that bring them close to the Sun. As they heat up, their ice turns to vapor and they can grow spectacular tails.

SUN

EARTH

VENUS

MERCURY

Jupiter is a huge ball of lightweight gases. It has swirling clouds and storms that last for centuries.

Mars is smaller than Earth and farther from the Sun, but it's still the most Earth-like planet.

The Sun's gravity traps objects in orbit around it out to a distance of 10 trillion km (6.2 trillion miles).

DID YOU KNOW? The asteroid belt between Mars and Jupiter contains about 1.5 million space rocks that are bigger than 1 km (0.6 miles) across.

Stars and the Galaxy

Our Sun is just one of 200 billion stars in a vast, slowly spinning spiral galaxy called the Milky Way. The Sun is a very average star and only appears bright because it is nearby. Other stars are so far that their light takes many years to reach Earth.

Types of Star

A star's brightness in the sky depends on its distance from Earth and how much light energy it's producing. Stars shine from nuclear fusion reactions that can last for billions of years. They vary from lower-energy dwarfs, 50,000 times fainter than the Sun, to giants 30 million times brighter.

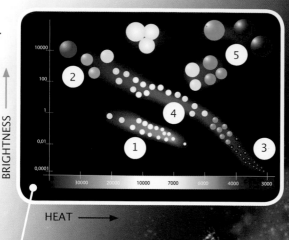

This graph shows the kinds of star at different temperatures and brightnesses. Red stars are cooler and blue ones are hotter.

KEY TO STAR TYPES
1. WHITE DWARFS
2. BLUE GIANTS
3. RED DWARFS
4. SUNLIKE STARS
5. RED SUPERGIANTS

How Stars Die

When a star runs out of nuclear fuel in its core, it goes through a series of changes as it dies. First it grows in size and brightens, becoming a red giant. All but the heaviest stars then puff off their outer layers, leaving behind a burned-out core called a white dwarf.

The most massive stars die in an explosion called a supernova that can briefly outshine an entire galaxy. All that's left of the star is an expanding bubble of superhot gas.

Scientists: Ejnar Hertzsprung, Henry Norris Russell
Discovery: Types of stars
Date: 1910–1913
The story: Hertzsprung and Russell found that nearly all stars follow a simple rule—the brighter they are, the hotter they are. Only a few stars are bright but cool (red giants) or faint but hot (white dwarfs).

AMAZING DISCOVERY

The Milky Way is about 120,000 light-years across. Our solar system orbits its core every 240 million years.

At the heart of the Milky Way, billions of red and yellow stars orbit a huge black hole.

The Milky Way is a huge flattened disc of gas, dust, and stars. New stars are born in spiral regions that wind their way out from the galaxy's core.

Stars form from collapsing clouds of gas. They begin their lives in clusters of hot blue and white stars.

DID YOU KNOW? Astronomers measure the distance to stars in light-years—how far light travels in a year. One light-year is 9.5 trillion km (5.9 trillion miles).

The Universe

Spiral galaxies appear blue and white because of the young, bright stars in their discs.

The Universe is (probably) everything that exists—a vast and perhaps endless expanse of space and time. Our Milky Way is just one of more than 100 billion galaxies. Powerful telescopes let us see millions of these galaxies spread out across space.

Measuring the Universe

Astronomers can work out how far away other galaxies are by looking for stars called variables. These stars change their brightness over time and some follow a repeating cycle. We can compare the variable's true brightness with how bright it appears to work out its distance—usually many millions of light-years. Another method is to look for exploding stars or supernovae in distant galaxies, and see how bright they get.

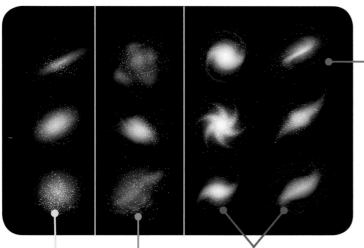

Elliptical galaxies

Irregular galaxies

Spiral galaxies

Galaxies have many shapes. Most of them are spirals like our Milky Way, ball-shaped ones called ellipticals, or shapeless clouds of gas called irregulars.

Cosmic Expansion

When astronomers first worked out the true distance to nearby galaxies, they noticed a pattern—the farther away a galaxy is, the faster it is moving away from us. This is because space itself is expanding, carrying galaxies away from each other like the raisins in a rising fruit cake.

Astronomers discovered the motion of stars and galaxies by measuring the "red shift" in their light. An object moving away from Earth has its light stretched to longer, redder wavelengths, while one moving toward us appears "blue shifted."

DID YOU KNOW? Looking across space is the same as looking back in time—the light we detect from the most distant galaxies has been on its way to us for 13.4 billion years.

Distant galaxies look redder because they're moving away more quickly—their light is stretched out.

Giant black holes in the cores of some galaxies fire jets of high-energy particles into intergalactic space.

Galaxies look different depending on the angle we're looking at them—this is a spiral viewed side-on.

Elliptical galaxies are balls of mostly red and yellow stars.

AMAZING DISCOVERY

Scientists: Henrietta Swan Leavitt (left), Edwin Hubble
Discovery: The scale of the Universe
Date: 1908–1929
The story: Leavitt was the first to spot the link between how some variable stars change over time and their true brightness. Hubble used this to estimate the distance of nearby galaxies, and to discover cosmic expansion.

The Big Bang and Beyond

The Universe was born out of a huge explosion that took place about 13.8 billion years ago. This Big Bang released huge amounts of energy that made all the matter in the Universe. It even created space and time themselves.

Evidence for the Big Bang

The discovery that all galaxies are moving apart shows that they must have been much closer together in the distant past, when the Universe would have been much denser and hotter. We can even see the faint afterglow of the Big Bang—waves of cosmic microwave background radiation (CMBR).

The CMBR is a faint glow of radio waves that comes from all over the sky. Brighter and darker areas show the seeds of galaxy clusters in the early Universe.

Will the Universe Ever End?

The Universe has three possible futures. Gravity from all the matter within it could slow its expansion and pull everything back to a Big Crunch. Another idea is that a mysterious force called dark energy could push everything apart in a Big Rip. Finally, space might just keep on expanding.

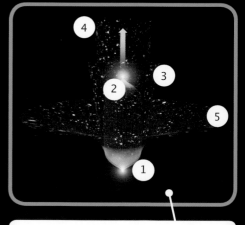

The Universe began with the Big Bang (1). It may end in an explosive Big Crunch (2) or keep expanding (3). This illustration also shows what would happen if the Universe had no dark energy (4) or if it had so much (5) that it would eventually tear itself apart in a Big Rip.

After a dark age lasting 200 million years, gas clouds collapsed to form the first stars and galaxies.

Earth and its solar system formed about 4.6 billion years ago.

The Milky Way galaxy is about ten billion years old.

A force called dark energy seems to be speeding up the Universe.

AMAZING DISCOVERY

Scientists: Arno Penzias, Robert Wilson
Discovery: Cosmic microwave background radiation (CMBR)
Date: 1964
The story: Astronomers had proposed that the Big Bang might have left faint radiation behind. Penzias and Wilson found it by accident when, testing a new radio antenna, they found a strange glow coming from all over the sky.

DID YOU KNOW? CMBR warms the entire Universe to just 2.7°C (37°F) above the coldest possible temperature, –273.15°C (–459.67°F) or absolute zero.

Glossary

ALLOY
A mixture of two or more metals, or of a metal and a non-metal.

AMPLITUDE
The height of a wave.

ANALOG
Using signals or information that are in a physical form, such as electric current or radio waves, which keeps changing.

ATOM
The smallest unit of an element.

BINARY
A base-2 system of numbering—it has only two numbers, 0 and 1. (Our usual numbering system is base-10: 0, 1, 2, 3, 4, 5, 6, 7, 8, 9.)

CELL
The smallest unit of a living body.

CHEMICAL BOND
A connection formed between two or more atoms that can only be broken by a stronger chemical reaction.

COMPOUND
A form of matter made up of elements bound together by chemical bonds.

CONVECTION
The process that moves heat around in a liquid or gas as hot areas expand and rise, and cold ones sink.

CRYSTAL
A form of solid material whose atoms or molecules are arranged in a repeating, regular pattern.

DIGITAL
Using signals or information that are in a coded form, usually binary.

DNA (deoxyribonucleic acid)
A substance with the structure of a double helix that carries genes and is found in the nucleus of cells in all living things.

ELECTRIC CHARGE
A property of some forms of matter that means they can be influenced by electromagnetism.

ELECTRICITY
A flow of electric charge from one place to another. It can be harnessed to do work.

ELECTROMAGNETISM
A basic force of nature that influences all particles that carry electric charge or a magnetic field.

ELECTRON
A negatively-charged subatomic particle, located outside the nucleus. Electricity is mostly driven by the flow of electrons from one place to another.

ELECTRONICS
A technology that uses the flow of very small electric currents to store, send, and alter information.

ELEMENT
A substance that is made entirely from one type of atom. The 118 elements found so far are listed in the periodic table.

ENERGY
What allows us to do work. It comes in many forms, including heat, light, electricity, and nuclear.

ENZYME
A protein that controls a chemical reaction.

EVOLUTION
The process by which living organisms gradually change over very long periods of time and that gives rise to new species. It is driven by natural selection.

FORCE
A push or pull on another object that changes its movement.

FRICTION
A force between moving objects, where their surfaces rub against each other, slowing them down.

GAS
A phase of matter in which atoms or molecules are widely separated and move freely.

GENE
An instruction on a section of a DNA molecule that is needed to make the structures and provide the functions that a living organism requires.

GRAVITY
A force that draws objects that have mass toward each other.

ISOTOPE
One of two or more special forms of atom belonging to the same element, but having varying numbers of neutrons.

LIGHT WAVE
An electromagnetic wave emitted or reflected from most objects. Our eyes use light to see the objects that surround us.

LIQUID
A phase of matter in which atoms or molecules are loosely bound together but can move freely.

LOGIC GATE
Part of a circuit in a computer that decides whether to allow current through, based on binary numbers.

MAGNETIC FIELD
A form of electromagnetism created around, and felt by, electrical conductors and metals with certain properties.

MATTER
Anything that has mass and occupies space.

MINERAL
A solid chemical compound, often with a crystal structure, formed from natural chemicals in water or the ground.

MOLECULE
The smallest unit of a compound, made up of two or more atoms bonded together.

NANOMETER
One-billionth of 1 m (3.3 ft).

NEUTRON
A subatomic particle with no charge, located inside the nucleus.

NUCLEUS
The middle of an atom, where its positive electric charge and nearly all of its mass are concentrated in a cluster of subatomic particles called protons and neutrons.

ORGAN
A collection of tissues in a complex living thing (usually an animal) that carries out a special function to help the organism survive.

ORGANELLE
A structure inside a cell that performs a particular job.

PHASE
The way the atoms or molecules of a substance are arranged.

PHOTON
A particle-like packet of light or other electromagnetic radiation.

PHOTOSYNTHESIS
A chemical reaction used by plants to make useful chemicals with energy from sunlight, carbon dioxide, and water.

PROTON
A positively-charged subatomic particle, located inside the nucleus.

QUANTUM PHYSICS
A branch of physics that describes how subatomic particles can sometimes behave like waves and show surprising properties.

RADIO WAVE
A moving wave of electromagnetic radiation with much less energy than light. Many technologies use radio waves to send and receive signals.

RADIOACTIVE
Relating to atoms whose nuclei are unstable and break apart, releasing high-energy particles.

REACTION
A chemical process that breaks apart chemical bonds within molecules, moves atoms around, and creates new molecules.

ROCK
A solid material found in nature, made up of a mix of minerals.

SOLID
A phase of matter in which atoms or molecules are tightly bound together and cannot move freely.

STAR
A huge ball of gas that produces energy, forcing small atomic nuclei together to form larger ones.

STRONG FORCE
A powerful force with a very short range that holds subatomic particles together in the nucleus of an atom.

SUBATOMIC PARTICLE
Any particle smaller than an atom. Many subatomic particles are themselves made from even smaller particles.

SUPERCONDUCTOR
A material that conducts electricity without losing its energy as heat.

SYSTEM
A group of linked organs, such as those in the digestive system, that work together to do a task.

TECTONICS
The very slow movement and rearrangement of blocks of Earth's outer rocky crust, which causes volcanoes and earthquakes.

TISSUE
A collection of cells that carries out a function in a living organism.

WAVE
A moving disturbance that carries energy from one place to another.

WEAK FORCE
A force found inside the atomic nucleus that allows subatomic particles to change some of their properties, producing radioactivity.

WORK
The process of moving energy from one place to another, usually through a force.

Index